Learn French with Short Stories

HypLern Interlinear Project
www.hyplern.com

Third edition: 2025, June

Author: Guy de Maupassant, Honoré de Balzac
Translation: Kees van den End
Foreword: Camilo Andrés Bonilla Carvajal PhD

ISBN: 978-1-989643-44-0

kees@hyplern.com
www.hyplern.com

Learn French with Short Stories

Interlinear French to English

Author
Guy de Maupassant, Honoré de Balzac

Translation
Kees van den End

HypLern Interlinear Project
www.hyplern.com

The HypLern Method

Learning a foreign language should not mean leafing through page after page in a bilingual dictionary until one's fingertips begin to hurt. Quite the contrary, through everyday language use, friendly reading, and direct exposure to the language we can get well on our way towards mastery of the vocabulary and grammar needed to read native texts. In this manner, learners can be successful in the foreign language without too much study of grammar paradigms or rules. Indeed, Seneca expresses in his sixth epistle that "Longum iter est per praecepta, breve et efficax per exempla[1]."

The HypLern series constitutes an effort to provide a highly effective tool for experiential foreign language learning. Those who are genuinely interested in utilizing original literary works to learn a foreign language do not have to use conventional graded texts or adapted versions for novice readers. The former only distort the actual essence of literary works, while the latter are highly reduced in vocabulary and relevant content. This collection aims to bring the lively experience of reading stories as directly told by their very authors to foreign language learners.

Most excited adult language learners will at some point seek their teachers' guidance on the process of learning to read in the foreign language rather than seeking out external opinions. However, both teachers and learners lack a general reading technique or strategy. Oftentimes, students undertake the reading task equipped with nothing more than a bilingual dictionary, a grammar book, and lots of courage. These efforts often end in frustration as the student builds mis-constructed nonsensical sentences after many hours spent on an aimless translation drill.

Consequently, we have decided to develop this series of interlinear translations intended to afford a comprehensive edition of unabridged texts. These texts are presented as they were originally written with no changes in word choice or order. As a result, we have a translated piece conveying the true meaning under every word from the original work. Our readers receive then two books in just one volume: the original version and its translation.

The reading task is no longer a laborious exercise of patiently decoding unclear and seemingly complex paragraphs. What's more, reading becomes an enjoyable and meaningful process of cultural, philosophical and linguistic learning. Independent learners can then acquire expressions and vocabulary while understanding pragmatic and socio-cultural dimensions of the target language by reading in it rather than reading about it.

Our proposal, however, does not claim to be a novelty. Interlinear translation is as old as the Spanish tongue, e.g. "glosses of [Saint] Emilianus", interlinear bibles in Old German, and of course James Hamilton's work in the 1800s. About the latter, we remind the readers, that as a revolutionary freethinker he promoted the publication of Greco-Roman classic works and further pieces in diverse languages. His effort, such as ours, sought to lighten the exhausting task of looking words up in large glossaries as an educational practice: "if there is any thing which fills reflecting men with melancholy and regret, it is the waste of mortal time, parental money, and puerile happiness, in the present method of pursuing Latin and Greek[2]".

Additionally, another influential figure in the same line of thought as Hamilton was John Locke. Locke was also the philosopher and translator of the Fabulae AEsopi in an interlinear plan. In 1600, he was already suggesting that interlinear texts, everyday communication, and use of the target language could be the most appropriate ways to achieve language learning:

> ...the true and genuine Way, and that which I would propose, not only as the easiest and best, wherein a Child might, without pains or Chiding, get a Language which others are wont to be whipt for at School six or seven Years together...[3]

---

1 "The journey is long through precepts, but brief and effective through examples". Seneca, Lucius Annaeus. (1961) Ad Lucilium Epistulae Morales, vol. I. London: W. Heinemann.

2 In: Hamilton, James (1829?) History, principles, practice and results of the Hamiltonian system, with answers to the Edinburgh and Westminster reviews; A lecture delivered at Liverpool; and instructions for the use of the books published on the system. Londres: W. Aylott and Co., 8, Pater Noster Row. p. 29.

3 In: Locke, John. (1693) Some thoughts concerning education. Londres: A. and J. Churchill. pp. 196-7.

Who can benefit from this edition?

We identify three kinds of readers, namely, those who take this work as a search tool, those who want to learn a language by reading authentic materials, and those attempting to read writers in their original language. The HypLern collection constitutes a very effective instrument for all of them.

1. For the first target audience, this edition represents a search tool to connect their mother tongue with that of the writer's. Therefore, they have the opportunity to read over an original literary work in an enriching and certain manner.
2. For the second group, reading every word or idiomatic expression in its actual context of use will yield a strong association between the form, the collocation, and the context. This will have a direct impact on long term learning of passive vocabulary, gradually building genuine reading ability in the original language. This book is an ideal companion not only to independent learners but also to those who take lessons with a teacher. At the same time, the continuous feeling of achievement produced during the process of reading original authors both stimulates and empowers the learner to study[1].
3. Finally, the third kind of reader will notice the same benefits as the previous ones. The proximity of a word and its translation in our interlinear texts is a step further from other collections, such as the Loeb Classical Library. Although their works might be considered the most famous in this genre, the presentation of texts on opposite pages hinders the immediate link between words and their semantic equivalence in our native tongue (or one we have a strong mastery of).

---

1 Some further ways of using the present work include:

1. As you progress through the stories, focus less on the lower line (the English translation). Instead, try to read through the upper line, staying in the foreign language as long as possible.
2. Even if you find glosses or explanatory footnotes about the mechanics of the language, you should make your own hypotheses on word formation and syntactical functions in a sentence. Feel confident about inferring your own language rules and test them progressively. You can also take notes concerning those idiomatic expressions or special language usage that calls your attention for later study.
3. As soon as you finish each text, check the reading in the original version (with no interlinear or parallel translation). This will fulfil the main goal of this

collection: bridging the gap between readers and original literary works, training them to read directly and independently.

Why interlinear?

Conventionally speaking, tiresome reading in tricky and exhausting circumstances has been the common definition of learning by texts. This collection offers a friendly reading format where the language is not a stumbling block anymore. Contrastively, our collection presents a language as a vehicle through which readers can attain and understand their authors' written ideas.

While learning to read, most people are urged to use the dictionary and distinguish words from multiple entries. We help readers skip this step by providing the proper translation based on the surrounding context. In so doing, readers have the chance to invest energy and time in understanding the text and learning vocabulary; they read quickly and easily like a skilled horseman cantering through a book.

Thereby we stress the fact that our proposal is not new at all. Others have tried the same before, coming up with evident and substantial outcomes. Certainly, we are not pioneers in designing interlinear texts. Nonetheless, we are nowadays the only, and doubtless, the best, in providing you with interlinear foreign language texts.

Handling instructions

Using this book is very easy. Each text should be read at least three times in order to explore the whole potential of the method. The first phase is devoted to comparing words in the foreign language to those in the mother tongue. This is to say, the upper line is contrasted to the lower line as the following example shows:

Et	Walter	Schnaffs	pleurait	quelquefois.
And	Walter	Schnaffs	cried	sometimes

The second phase of reading focuses on capturing the meaning and sense of the original text. As readers gain practice with the method, they should be able to focus on the target language without getting distracted by the translation. New users of the method, however, may find it helpful to cover the translated lines with a piece of paper as illustrated in the image below. Subsequently, they try to understand the meaning of every word, phrase, and entire sentences in the target language itself, drawing on the translation only when necessary. In this phase, the reader should resist the temptation to look at the translation for every word. In doing so, they will find that they are able to understand a good portion of the text by reading directly in the target language, without the crutch of the translation. This is the skill we are looking to train: the ability to read and understand native materials and enjoy them as native speakers do, that being, directly in the original language.

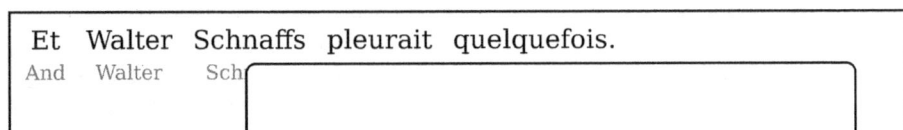

> Et   Walter   Schnaffs   pleurait   quelquefois.
> And   Walter   Sch

In the final phase, readers will be able to understand the meaning of the text when reading it without additional help. There may be some less common words and phrases which have not cemented themselves yet in the reader's brain, but the majority of the story should not pose any problems. If desired, the reader can use an SRS or some other memorization method to learning these straggling words.

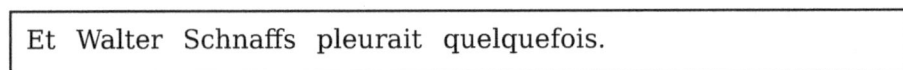

> Et   Walter   Schnaffs   pleurait   quelquefois.

Above all, readers will not have to look every word up in a dictionary to read a text in the foreign language. This otherwise wasted time will be spent concentrating on their principal interest. These new readers will tackle authentic texts while learning their vocabulary and expressions to use in further communicative (written or oral) situations. This book is just one work from an overall series with the same purpose. It really helps those who are afraid of having "poor vocabulary" to feel confident about reading directly in the language. To all of them and to all of you, welcome to the amazing experience of living a foreign language!

Additional tools

Check out shop.hyplern.com or contact us at info@hyplern.com for free mp3s (if available) and free empty (untranslated) versions of the eBooks that we have on offer.

For some of the older eBooks and paperbacks we have Windows, iOS and Android apps available that, next to the interlinear format, allow for a pop-up format, where hovering over a word or clicking on it gives you its meaning. The apps also have any mp3s, if available, and integrated vocabulary practice.

Visit the site hyplern.com for the same functionality online. This is where we will be working non-stop to make all our material available in multiple formats, including audio where available, and vocabulary practice.

Table of Contents

L'aventure de Walter Schnaffs I
The Adventure of Walter Schnaffs I

Maupassant-- L'aventure de Walter Schnaffs I
Maupassant the Adventure of Walter Schnaffs I

Depuis son entrée en France avec l'armée
Since his entry in France with the army

d'invasion, Walter Schnaffs se jugeait le plus
of invasion Walter Schnaffs himself judged the most

malheureux des hommes. Il était gros, marchait
unhappy of the men He was fat marched
of

avec peine, soufflait beaucoup et souffrait
with difficulty breathed heavily a lot and suffered

affreusement des pieds qu'il avait fort plats et
terribly of the feet that he had very flat and
which were

fort gras. Il était en outre pacifique et
very fat He was in besides peaceful and
in addition

bienveillant, nullement magnanime ou sanguinaire,
benevolent by no means noble or bloodthirsty

père de quatre enfants qu'il adorait et marié
father of four children that he adored and married

avec une jeune femme blonde, dont il regrettait
with a young woman blond of which he missed

désespérément chaque soir les tendresses, les
hopelessly every evening the tendernesses the

petits soins et les baisers.
small cares and the kisses

Il aimait se lever tard et se coucher tôt,
He liked himself raise late and himself lay down early
to get up to go to bed

manger lentement de bonnes choses et boire de
to eat slow of good things and to drink -of-

la bière dans les brasseries.
-the- beer in the breweries
bars

Il songeait en outre que tout ce qui est doux
He thought in besides that all this what is soft
in addition

dans l'existence disparaît avec la vie; et il
in the existence disappears with the life and he

3

gardait au coeur une haine épouvantable,
kept with the heart a hatred terrible

instinctive et raisonnée en même temps, pour
instinctive and reasoned at same time for
at the

les canons, les fusils, les revolvers et les
-the- cannons -the- guns -the- revolvers and -the-

sabres, mais surtout pour les baïonnettes, se
sabres but especially for -the- bayonets himself

sentant incapable de manoeuvrer assez vivement
feeling incapable of moving enough lively
quickly

cette arme rapide pour défendre son gros ventre.
this weapon rapid for to defend his large belly

Et, quand il se couchait sur la terre, la nuit
And when he himself lay down on the ground the night
went to sleep

venue, roulé dans son manteau à côté des
arrived rolled in his coat at side of the

camarades qui ronflaient, il pensait longuement
comrades who snored he thought a long time

aux siens laissés là-bas et aux dangers
about the / about his people left down there and of the dangers

semés sur sa route: S'il était tué, que
sown on his road If he was killed what

deviendraient les petits? Qui donc les nourrirait
would become of the little ones Who then them would nourish

et les élèverait? A l'heure même, ils n'étaient
and them would raise At the hour even they were not

pas riches, malgré les dettes qu'il avait
not rich in spite of the debts that he had

contractées en partant pour leur laisser quelque
contracted in leaving / when leaving for them to leave some

argent.
money

Et Walter Schnaffs pleurait quelquefois.
And Walter Schnaffs cried sometimes

Au commencement des batailles il se sentait
At the beginning of the battles he himself felt / felt

dans les jambes de telles faiblesses qu'il se
in the legs -of- such weaknesses that he himself

serait laissé tomber, s'il n'avait songé que toute
would let fall if he did not have thought that all

l'armée lui passerait sur le corps. Le sifflement
the army him would pass over the body The whistling

des balles hérissait le poil sur sa peau. Depuis
of the bullets raised the hair on his skin Since

des mois il vivait ainsi dans la terreur et
-of the- months he lived like this in -the- terror and

dans l'angoisse. Son corps d'armée s'avançait vers
in anguish His body of army advanced towards
group

la Normandie, et il fut un jour envoyé en
-the- Normandy and he was one day send in

reconnaissance avec un faible détachement qui
reconaissance with a weak detachment that

devait simplement explorer une partie du pays
had simply to explore one part of the country

et se replier ensuite. Tout semblait calme
and itself fold up again afterwards All seemed calm
to return

dans la campagne; rien n'indiquait une
in the countryside nothing not indicated a
indicated

résistance préparée.
resistance prepared

Or, les Prussiens descendaient avec tranquillité
However the Prussians descended with calmness

dans une petite vallée que coupaient des ravins
in a small valley that cut of the ravines
the

profonds, quand une fusillade violente les arrêta
deep when a shooting violent them stopped

net, jetant bas une vingtaine des leurs; et une
cleanly throwing low one score of the theirs and a
of

troupe de francs-tireurs, sortant brusquement
troop of free-shooters leaving suddenly
{French irregular military}

d'un petit bois grand comme la main, s'élança
of a small wood large like the hand sprang
a

en avant, la baïonnette au fusil.
in forward the bayonet at the rifle
  forth

Walter Schnaffs demeura d'abord immobile,
Walter Schnaffs remained from start motionless
                initially

tellement surpris et éperdu qu'il ne pensait
so much surprised and dazed that he not thought

même pas à fuir. Puis un désir fou de détaler
even -not- to flee Then a desire insane of to bolt

le saisit;
him seized

mais il songea aussitôt qu'il courait comme une
but he thought at once that he ran like a

tortue en comparaison des maigres Français qui
tortoise in comparison of the thin French who
                to the

arrivaient en bondissant comme un troupeau de
arrived in leaping like a herd of
         leaping

chèvres. Alors, apercevant à six pas devant lui
goats Then seeing at six steps in front of him

un large fossé plein de broussailles couvertes de
a broad ditch full of undergrowth covered of

feuilles sèches, il y sauta à pieds joints,
leaves dry he there jumped with feet joint

sans songer même à la profondeur, comme on
without to think even at the depth like one
of

saute d'un pont dans une rivière. Il passa, à la
jumps of a bridge in a river He passed at the

façon d'une flèche, à travers une couche épaisse
manner of an arrow -to- through a layer thick

de lianes et de ronces aiguës qui lui déchirèrent
of vines and of brambles sharp that him tore

la face et les mains, et il tomba lourdement
the face and the hands and he fell heavily

assis sur un lit de pierres.
sat on a bed of stones

Levant aussitôt les yeux, il vit le ciel par le
Raising at once the eyes he saw the sky through the

trou qu'il avait fait.
hole that he had made

Ce trou révélateur le pouvait dénoncer, et il
This hole revealing him could denounce and he

se traîna avec précaution, à quatre pattes, au
himself trailed with precaution on four paws at the
on hands and feet

fond de cette ornière, sous le toit de branchages
bottom of this rut under the roof of branches

enlacés, allant le plus vite possible, en
intertwined going the most quick possible in

s'éloignant du lieu de combat.
moving himself away from the place of fight
of the

Puis il s'arrêta et s'assit de nouveau, tapi
Then he stopped and sat down of new hidden
of new (again)

comme un lièvre au milieu des hautes herbes
like one hare in the middle of the high grass

sèches.
dry

Il entendit pendant quelque temps encore des
He heard during some time still -of the

détonations, des cris et des plaintes.
detonations -of the- cries and -of the- begging

Puis les clameurs de la lutte s'affaiblirent,
Then the clamours of the fight weakened

cessèrent. Tout redevint muet et calme.
ceased All became again quiet and calm

Soudain quelque chose remua: contre lui. Il eut
Suddenly some thing stirred against him He had
something

un sursaut épouvantable. C'était un petit oiseau
a start terrible It was a small bird

qui, s'étant posé sur une branche, agitait des
who itself being perched on a branch moved of the
the

feuilles mortes.
leaves dead

Pendant près d'une heure, le coeur de Walter
During near of one hour the heart of Walter

Schnaffs en battit à grands coups pressés.
Schnaffs in beat with large blows pressed
there

La nuit venait, emplissant d'ombre le ravin. Et
The night came filling up of shade the ravine And

le soldat se mit à songer. Qu'allait-il faire?
the soldier himself put to think What went he to do
What should he

Qu'allait-il devenir? Rejoindre son armée? Mais
What went he become To rejoin his army But
What should he

comment? Mais par où? Et il lui faudrait
how But by where And it him would be necessary

recommencer l'horrible vie d'angoisses,
to start again the horrible life of anguishes

d'épouvantes, de fatigues et de souffrances qu'il
of terrors of exhaustions and of sufferings that he

menait depuis le commencement de la guerre!
led since the beginning of the war

Non! Il ne se sentait plus ce courage. Il
No He not himself felt more this courage He

n'aurait plus l'énergie qu'il fallait pour
would not have anymore the energy that he needed to

supporter les marches et affronter les dangers de
support the marches and to face the dangers of

toutes les minutes.
all the minutes

Mais que faire?
But what to do

Il ne pouvait rester dans ce ravin et
He not could to remain in this ravine and

s'y cacher jusqu'à la fin des hostilités.
himself there hide until the end of the hostilities
himself there hide

Non, certes. S'il n'avait pas fallu manger, cette
Not assuredly If he had not -not- needed to eat this

perspective ne l'aurait pas trop atterré; mais
prospect not would have -not- too much dismayed but

il fallait manger, manger tous les jours.
it was necessary to eat to eat all the days

Et il se trouvait ainsi tout seul, en armes, en
And he himself found thus all alone in weapons in
armed

uniforme, sur le territoire ennemi, loin de ceux
uniform on the territory enemy far of those

qui le pouvaient défendre. Des frissons lui
who him could defend Of the shivers him
Shivers

couraient sur la peau.
ran over the skin

Soudain il pensa: 'Si seulement j'étais prisonnier!'
Suddenly he thought If only I was prisoner

Et son coeur frémit de désir, d'un désir violent,
And his heart shook of desire of a desire violent

immodéré, d'être prisonnier des Français.
immoderate to be prisoner of the French

Prisonnier! Il serait sauvé, nourri, logé, à
Prisoner He would be saved nourished placed at

l'abri des balles et des sabres, sans
the shelter of the bullets and of the sabres without

appréhension possible, dans une bonne prison bien
apprehension possible in a good prison well

gardée. Prisonnier! Quel rêve!
kept Prisoner What (a) dream

Et sa résolution fut prise immédiatement:
And his decision was taken immediately

"Je vais me constituer prisonnier."
I go myself to constitute prisoner

Il se leva, résolu à exécuter ce projet sans
He himself raised resolute to carry out this project without

tarder d'une minute. Mais il demeura immobile,
delay of a minute But he remained motionless

assailli soudain par des réflexions fâcheuses et
assailed suddenly by -of the- reflexions annoying and

par des terreurs nouvelles.
by -of the- terrors new

Où allait-il se constituer prisonnier?
Where went-he himself to constitute prisoner
would he

Comment? De quel côté?
How   Of   which   side

Et   des   images affreuses,   des   images de mort,
And   -of the-   images   dreadful   -of the-   images   of   death

se   précipitèrent dans son âme.
themselves   rushed   in   his   mind
       rushed

Il   allait   courir   des   dangers   terribles   en
He   went   to run   -of the-   dangers   terrible   in

s'aventurant seul, avec son casque à pointe,   par
  venturing   alone with   his   helmet   to   point   through
                           pointed

la   campagne.
the   countryside

S'il   rencontrait   des   paysans?   Ces   paysans,
If he   met   -of the-   peasants   These   peasants

voyant   un   Prussien   perdu,   un   Prussien   sans
seeing   a   Prussian   lost   a   Prussian   without

défense,   le   tueraient comme un chien errant!
defense   him   would kill   like   a   dog   stray

Ils le massacreraient avec leurs fourches, leurs
They him would massacre with their forks their

pioches, leurs faux, leurs pelles! Ils en
pickaxes their scythes their shovels They of him

feraient une bouillie, une pâtée, avec
would make a pulp a paté with

l'acharnement des vaincus exaspérés.
the eagerness of the vanquished exasperated
desperate

S'il rencontrait des francs-tireurs? Ces
If he met -of the- free-shooters These

francs-tireurs, des enragés sans loi ni
free-shooters -of the- enraged without law nor

discipline, le fusilleraient pour s'amuser, pour
discipline him would shoot for to have fun for

passer une heure, histoire de rire en voyant sa
to pass a hour story of to laugh in seeing his
as a joke aiming for

tête. Et il se croyait déjà appuyé contre un
head And he himself believed already put up against a

mur en face de douze canons de fusils, dont les
wall in front of twelve barrels of rifles of which the
    in front of

petits trous ronds et noirs semblaient le
small holes round and black seemed him

regarder.
to look at

S'il rencontrait l'armée française elle-même?
If he met the army French itself

Les hommes d'avant-garde le prendraient pour un
The men of front guard him would take for a
    of the vanguard

éclaireur, pour quelque hardi et malin troupier
scout for some bold and malignant trouper

parti seul en reconnaissance, et ils lui tireraient
parted alone in reconnaissance and they him would shoot

dessus.
  above
down

Et il entendait déjà les détonations irrégulières
And he heard already the detonations irregular

des soldats couchés dans les broussailles, tandis
of the soldiers hidden in the undergrowth while

que lui, debout au milieu d'un champ, affaissait,
that he upright in the middle of a field collapsed

troué comme une écumoire par les balles qu'il
perforated like a skimmer by the bullets that he

sentait entrer dans sa chair.
felt to enter in his flesh

Il se rassit, désespéré. Sa situation lui
He himself sat again despaired His situation him

paraissait sans issue.
appeared without exit

L'aventure de Walter Schnaffs II
The Adventure of Walter Schnaffs II

Maupassant-- L'aventure de Walter Schnaffs II
Maupassant   the Adventure of   Walter   Schnaffs   II

La nuit était tout à fait venue, la nuit muette
The night   was   all to done arrived the night   silent
          had   wholly

et noire. Il ne bougeait plus. Tressaillant à
and black He not   moved   (any)more Trembling   at

tous les bruits inconnus et légers qui passent
all   the   noises unknown and slight   that   pass

dans les ténèbres. Un lapin, tapant du cul
in   the darknesses A rabbit peeking out of the hole
        darkness

au bord d'un terrier, faillit faire s'enfuir
at the edge of a   burrow failed to make -himself- flee
                 almost   made

Walter Schnaffs. Les cris des chouettes lui
Walter Schnaffs The cries of the   owls   him

déchiraient l'âme, le traversant de peurs
tore · the soul · him · traversing · of / with · fear

soudaines, douloureuses comme des blessures. Il
sudden · painful · like · -of the- · wounds · He

écarquillait ses gros yeux pour tâcher de voir
opened wide · his · large · eyes · to · try · -of- · to see

dans l'ombre; et il s'imaginait à tout moment
in · the shadow / the shadows · and · he · thought · at · every · moment

entendre marcher près de lui.
to hear · walking · near · of · him

Après d'interminables heures et des angoisses
After · of interminable / endless · hours · and · -of the- · fears

de damné, il aperçut, à travers son plafond
of · (the) damned · he · saw · -to- · through · his · ceiling

de branchages, le ciel qui devenait clair.
of · branches · the · sky · which · became · clear

Alors, un soulagement immense le pénétra; ses
Then · a · relief · immense · him · penetrated · his

membres   se   détendirent, reposés soudain;
members   themselves   slackened   rested   suddenly

son coeur s'apaisa; ses yeux   se   fermèrent.
his   heart   calmed down   his   eyes   themselves   closed
                                                  closed

Il s'endormit.
He   fell asleep

Quand il   se   réveilla, le soleil lui   parut arrivé
When   he   himself   woke up   the   sun   him   appeared   arrived
                    awoke

à peu près   au   milieu   du   ciel; il   devait   être
to little near   at the   middle   of the   sky   it   had   to be
    almost   in the

midi.
noon

Aucun bruit   ne   troublait   la   paix   morne   des
No   noise   -not-   disturbed   the   peace   dull   of the

champs;   et   Walter   Schnaffs   s'aperçut   qu'il   était
fields   and   Walter   Schnaffs   realized   that he   was
                                                       had

atteint d'une   faim   aiguë.
reached   of a   hunger   acute
acquired   a

Il bâillait, la bouche humide à la pensée du
He yawned the mouth moist at the thought of the

saucisson des soldats; et son estomac lui faisait
sausage of the soldiers and his stomach him made

mal.
sick

Il se leva, fit quelques pas, sentit que ses
He himself raised made some steps felt that his
    got up

jambes étaient faibles, et se rassit pour
legs were weak and himself sat again for
    sat down again

réfléchir. Pendant deux ou trois heures encore, il
to think During two or three hours still he

établit le pour et le contre, changeant à
drew up the for and the against changing at
    advantages disadvantages

tout moment de résolution, combattu, malheureux,
every moment of decision fought unhappy

tiraillé par les raisons les plus contraires.
pulled about by the reasons the most opposite

Une idée lui parut enfin logique et pratique,
An idea him appeared finally logical and practical

c'était de guetter le passage d'un villageois seul,
it was of to watch for the passage of a villager alone

sans armes, et sans outils de travail dangereux,
without weapons and without tools of work dangerous

de courir au-devant de lui et de se remettre
of to run at the front of him and of himself put over
           in front   to turn himself over

en ses mains en lui faisant bien comprendre
in his hands in him making well to understand
                while

qu'il se rendait. Alors il ôta son casque,
that he himself gave over Then he removed his helmet
         gave himself up

dont la pointe le pouvait trahir, et il sortit
of which the point him could betray and he stuck out

sa tête au bord de son trou, avec des
his head at the edge of his hole with -of the-
          from the

précautions infinies.
precautions infinite

Aucun être isolé ne se montrait à l'horizon.
No   being isolated -not- itself   showed   at the horizon
       No one

Là-bas,   à droite, un petit village envoyait au
There-down to (the) right a   small village   sent   to the
 Over there

ciel la fumée de ses toits, la fumée de ses
sky the smoke of its roofs the smoke of its

cuisines!
kitchens

Là-bas,   à gauche; il apercevait, au bout des
There-down at (the) left he   saw   at the end of the
 Over there

arbres d'une avenue, un grand château flanqué de
trees of an avenue a large castle flanked by

tourelles.
turrets

Il attendit jusqu'au soir, souffrant affreusement,
He waited until the evening suffering terribly

ne voyant rien que des vols de corbeaux,
not seeing nothing but -of the- flights of crows

n'entendant rien que les plaintes sourdes de ses
not hearing nothing but the complaints muffled of his

entrailles.
entrails

Et la nuit encore tomba sur lui.
And the night again fell over him

Il s'allongea au fond de sa retraite et il
He himself stretched out at the bottom of his hide out and he

s'endormit d'un sommeil fiévreux, hanté de
fell asleep of a sleep feverish haunted of
with a

cauchemars, d'un sommeil d'homme affamé.
nightmares of a sleep of man famished
of a man

L'aurore se leva de nouveau sur sa tête. Il
The dawn itself raised of new over his head He
came up again

se remit en observation.
himself set back in observation
set himself again to

Mais la campagne restait vide comme la
But the countryside remained empty like the

veille; et une peur nouvelle entrait dans
evening before · and · a · fear · new · entered · in

l'esprit de Walter Schnaffs, la peur de mourir de
the spirit · of · Walter · Schnaffs · the · fear · of · to die · of

faim!
hunger

Il se voyait étendu au fond de son trou,
He · himself · saw · spread out · at the · bottom · of · his · hole

sur le dos, les deux yeux fermés.
on · the · back · the · two · eyes · closed

Puis des bêtes, des petites bêtes de toute
Then · -of the- · animals · -of the- · small · animals · of · all

sorte s'approchaient de son cadavre et se
sorts · approached · -of- · his · corpse · and · themselves

mettaient à le manger, l'attaquant partout à la
put · to · him · eat · him attacking · everywhere · at · the

fois, se glissant sous ses vêtements
(same) time · themselves · slipping · under · his · clothing

pour mordre sa peau froide. Et un grand corbeau
for to bite his skin cold And a large crow

lui piquait les yeux de son bec effilé.
him picked the eyes of its beak sharpened
with

Alors, il devint fou, s'imaginant qu'il allait
Then he became crazy thinking that he went

s'évanouir de faiblesse et ne plus pouvoir
to faint of weakness and not anymore to be able

marcher. Et déjà, il s'apprêtait à s'élancer
to go And already he himself prepared to launch himself

vers le village, résolu à tout oser, à tout
towards the village decided to everything dare to all

braver, quand il aperçut trois paysans qui
face when he saw three peasants who

s'en allaient aux champs avec leurs fourches
themselves in going to the fields with their hayforks
went

sur l'épaule, et il se replongea dans sa
on the shoulder and he himself plunged back in his

cachette.
hiding-place

Mais, dès que le soir obscurcit la plaine, il
But as soon as that the evening darkened the plain he

sortit lentement du fossé, et se mit en
got out slowly from the ditch and himself set on
started

route, courbé, craintif, le coeur battant, vers
(the) road bent apprehensive the heart beating towards

le château lointain, préférant entrer là-dedans
the castle in the distance preferring to enter there inside

plutôt qu'au village qui lui semblait redoutable
rather than at the village which him seemed frightening

comme une tanière pleine de tigres. Les fenêtres
like a den full of tigers The windows

d'en bas brillaient. Une d'elles était même
of in low shone One of them was even
of the lower floor

ouverte; et une forte odeur de viande cuite
opened and a strong smell of meat cooked

s'en échappait, une odeur qui pénétra
itself there escaped a smell which penetrated

brusquement dans le nez et jusqu'au fond du
abruptly in the nose and down to the bottom of the

ventre de Walter Schnaffs, qui le crispa, le fit
belly of Walter Schnaffs which him tensed up him let

haleter, l'attirant irrésistiblement, lui jetant au
pant him attracting irresistibly him throwing to the

coeur une audace désespérée.
heart an audacity despaired

Et brusquement, sans réfléchir, il apparut,
And abruptly without to reflect he appeared

casqué, dans le cadre de la fenêtre.
helmeted in the frame of the window

Huit domestiques dînaient autour d'une grande
Eight servants dined around of a large

table. Mais soudain une bonne demeura
table But suddenly one good man remained

béante,   **laissant tomber son verre, les yeux**
gaping   letting   to fall   his   glass   the   eyes
mouth wide open

fixes.
fixed

Tous les regards suivirent le sien!
All   the   stares   followed   -the-   his

On aperçut l'ennemi!
One   saw   the enemy
They

"Seigneur! les Prussiens attaquaient le château!"
Lord   the   Prussians   attacked   the   castle

Ce fut d'abord un cri, un seul cri, fait de huit
This was   initially   one   cry   a   lone   cry   made   of   eight

cris poussés sur huit tons différents, un cri
cries   uttered   on   eight   tones   different   a   cry

d'épouvante horrible, puis une levée tumultueuse,
of terror   horrible   then   a   raising   tumultuous

une bousculade mêlée, une fuite éperdue vers
a   scuffle   mixed   an   escape   desperate   towards

la   porte   du   fond.
the   door   of the   back

Les   chaises   tombaient,   les   hommes   renversaient   les
The⌢   chairs   fell   the   men   knocked down   the

femmes   et   passaient   dessus.
women   and   passed   over

En   deux   secondes,   la   pièce   fut   vide,   abandonnée,
In   two   seconds   the   room   was   empty   abandoned

avec   la   table   couverte   de   mangeaille   en   face   de
with   the   table   covered   with   foodstuffs   in   face   of
                                                before

Walter   Schnaffs   stupéfait,   toujours   debout   dans   sa
Walter   Schnaffs   stupefied   always   standing   in   the
                              still

fenêtre.
windows

Après   quelques   instants   d'hésitation,   il   enjamba   le
After   some   moments   of hesitation   he   legged   the
                                           climbed over

mur   d'appui   et   s'avança   vers   les   assiettes.
wall   of support   and   himself advanced   towards   the   plates
parapet

Sa faim exaspérée le faisait trembler comme un
His hunger exasperated him let tremble like a

fiévreux: mais une terreur le retenait, le
feverish person but a terror him retained him

paralysait encore. Il écouta. Toute la maison
paralysed still He listened Whole the house

semblait frémir; des portes se fermaient,
seemed to shake -of the- doors themselves closed
were closed

des pas rapides couraient sur le plancher de
-of the- steps quick ran on the floor of

dessus. Le Prussien inquiet tendait l'oreille à ces
above The Prussian anxious tended the ear to these

confuses rumeurs; puis il entendit des bruits
confused rumours then he heard -of the- noises

sourds comme si des corps fussent tombés dans
muffled as if -of the- bodies were fallen in
on

la terre molle, au pied des murs, des
the ground soft at the foot of the walls of the

corps humains sautant du premier étage.
bodies human jumping from the first floor
ground floor

Puis tout mouvement, toute agitation cessèrent, et
Then all movement all agitation ceased and

le grand château devint silencieux comme un
the large castle became silent like a

tombeau. Walter Schnaffs s'assit devant une
tomb Walter Schnaffs sat down in front of a

assiette restée intacte, et il se mit à manger.
plate remained intact and he himself set to eat
started

Il mangeait par grandes bouchées comme s'il eût
He ate by large mouthfuls as if he had

craint d'être interrompu trop tôt, de ne pouvoir
fear to be stopped too early of not to be able

engloutir assez. Il jetait à deux mains les
to absorb enough He threw with two hands the

morceaux dans sa bouche ouverte comme une
pieces in his mouth opened like a

trappe; et des paquets de nourriture lui
trap door / and / -of the- / packages / of / food / him

descendaient coup sur coup dans l'estomac,
descended / blow / on / blow / in / the stomach

gonflant sa gorge en passant. Parfois, il
inflating / his / throat / in / passing / Sometimes / he

s'interrompait, prêt à crever à la façon d'un
stopped / ready / to / burst / at / the / way / of a

tuyau trop plein.
pipe / too / full

Il prenait à la cruche au cidre et se
He / took / with the hold of / the / jug / of the / cider / and / himself

déblayait l'oesophage comme on lave un conduit
cleared / the oesophagus / like / one / washes / a / duct

bouché.
blocked

Il vida toutes les assiettes, tous les plats et
He / emptied / all / the / plates / all / the / dishes / and

toutes les bouteilles; puis, saoul de liquide et de
all the bottles then drunk of liquid and of

mangeaille, abruti, rouge, secoué par des
food dazed red shaken by -of the-

hoquets, l'esprit troublé et la bouche grasse, il
hiccups the spirit disturbed and the mouth greasy he

déboutonna son uniforme pour souffler, incapable
peeled off his uniform for to breath incompetent

d'ailleurs de faire un pas. Ses yeux
moreover of to make one step His eyes

se fermaient, ses idées s'engourdissaient; il
themselves closed his thoughts grew numb he
closed

posa son front pesant dans ses bras croisés sur la
posed his face heavy in his arms crossed on the

table, et il perdit doucement la notion des
table and he lost quietly the notion of the
of

choses et des faits.
things and of the facts
of

Le dernier croissant éclairait vaguement
The last crescent (moon) lit vaguely

l'horizon au-dessus des arbres du parc.
the horizon over the trees of the park

C'était l'heure froide qui précède le jour.
It was the hour cold that precede the day

Des ombres glissaient dans les fourrés, nombreuses
The shades slipped in the thickets many

et muettes; et parfois, un rayon de lune
and silent and sometimes a ray of (the) moon

faisait reluire dans l'ombre une pointe d'acier.
made glitter in the shade a point of steel

Le château tranquille dressait sa grande silhouette
The castle quiet drew up its large silhouette

noire. Deux fenêtres seules brillaient encore
black Two windows only shone still

au rez-de-chaussée. Soudain, une voix tonnante
at the level-of-road Suddenly a voice thundering
at the level of the road

hurla:
howled

"En avant! nom d'un nom! à l'assaut! mes
in forward name of a name to -the- attack my
Advance

enfants!"
children

Alors, en un instant, les portes, les contrevents et
Then in one moment the doors the shutters and

les vitres s'enfoncèrent sous un flot d'hommes
the panes were broken down under a flood of men

qui s'élança, brisa, creva tout, envahit la maison.
that launched broke burst all invaded the house

En un instant cinquante soldats armés jusqu'aux
In a moment fifty soldiers armed up to the

cheveux, bondirent dans la cuisine où reposait
hairs leaped in the kitchen where rested

pacifiquement Walter Schnaffs, et, lui posant sur
peacefully Walter Schnaffs and him posing on

la poitrine cinquante fusils chargés, le
the chest fifty rifles charged him

culbutèrent, le roulèrent, le saisirent, le lièrent
tumbled over him rolled over him seized him bound

des pieds à la tête.
from the feet to the head

Il haletait d'ahurissement, trop abruti pour
He panted of bewilderment too dazed for

comprendre, battu, crossé et fou de peur.
to understand beaten lugged and mad of fear

Et tout d'un coup, un gros militaire chamarré
And all of a blow a large soldier adorned
sudden

d'or lui planta son pied sur le ventre en
of gold him planted his foot on the belly while

vociférant:
vociferating

"Vous êtes mon prisonnier, rendez-vous!"
You are my prisoner give yourself up

39

Le Prussien n'entendit que ce seul mot
The Prussian did not understand but this only word

'prisonnier,' et il gémit:
prisoner and he groaned

"ya, ya, ya."
ya ya ya

Il fut relevé, ficelé sur une chaise, et examiné
He was raised up tied on a chair and examined

avec une vive curiosité par ses vainqueurs qui
with a lively curiosity by his winners who

soufflaient comme des baleines. Plusieurs
breathed heavily like -of the- whales Several

s'assirent, n'en pouvant plus d'émotion et de
sat down not in being able anymore of emotion and of

fatigue.
exhaustion

Il souriait, lui, il souriait maintenant, sûr d'être
He smiled him he smiled now sure of to be
he

---

enfin prisonnier!
finally prisoner

Un autre officier entra et prononça:
An other officer entered and pronounced

"Mon colonel, les ennemis se sont enfuis;
My colonel the enemies themselves are (have) fled

plusieurs semblent avoir été blessés. Nous restons
several seem to have been wounded We remain

maîtres de la place."
masters of the place

Le gros militaire qui s'essuyait le front vociféra:
The large soldier who wiped himself the face vociferated

"Victoire!"
Victoire

Et il écrivit sur un petit agenda de commerce
And he wrote on (in) a small diary of trade

tiré de sa poche:
pulled out of his pocket

'Après une lutte acharnée, les Prussiens ont dû
After a fight bloody the Prussians have had to

battre en retraite, emportant leurs morts et leurs
beat in retreat carrying their dead and their

blessés, qu'on évalue à cinquante hommes hors.'
wounded that one estimates at fifty men over

Le jeune officier reprit:
The young officer began again

"Quelles dispositions dois-je prendre, mon colonel?"
Which measures must I take my colonel

Le colonel répondit:
The colonel answered

"Nous allons nous replier pour éviter un retour
We let us go us to fold up for to avoid a return
pull back

offensif avec de l'artillerie et des forces
offensive with -of- the artillery and -of the- forces

supérieures."
superior

Et il donna l'ordre de repartir.
And he gave the order of to set out again

La colonne se reforma dans l'ombre, sous les
The column itself reformed in the shade under the

murs du château, et se mit en mouvement,
walls of the castle and itself put in movement

enveloppant de partout Walter Schnaffs garrotté,
surrounding from everywhere Walter Schnaffs tied up

tenu par six guerriers le revolver au poing.
held by six warriors the revolver at the fist
in the

Des reconnaissances furent envoyées pour éclairer
Of the reconnaissances were sent for to light
Reconaissances

la route. On avançait avec prudence, faisant halte
the road One advanced with prudence making halt
They

de temps en temps. Au jour levant, on arrivait à
of time in time At the day raising one arrived at
now and then they

la sous-préfecture de la Roche-Oysel, dont
the subprefecture of la Roche-Oysel of which

la garde nationale avait accompli ce fait d'armes.
the guard national had achieved this fact of arms

La population anxieuse et surexcitée attendait.
The population anxious and over-excited waited

Quand on aperçut le casque du prisonnier,
When one saw the helmet of the prisoner
people

des clameurs formidables éclatèrent.
-of the- clamours formidable erupted

Les femmes levaient les bras; des vieilles
The women raised the arms the old women

pleuraient; un aïeul lança sa béquille au
cried one grandfather launched his crutch at the

Prussien et blessa le nez d'un de ses gardiens.
Prussian and wounded the nose of one of his guards

Le colonel hurlait.
The colonel yelled

"Veillez à la sûreté du captif."
Take care at the safety of the prisoner
of

On parvint enfin à la maison de ville. La prison
One arrived finally at the house of city The prison
They   city hall

fut ouverte, et Walter Schnaffs jeté dedans, libre
was opened and Walter Schnaffs thrown inside free

de liens.
of bonds

Deux cents hommes en armes montèrent la
Two hundred men in arms set up the

garde autour du bâtiment.
guard around of the building
             of the

Alors, malgré des symptômes d'indigestion qui le
Then in spite of the symptoms of indigestion that him

tourmentaient depuis quelque temps, le Prussien,
tormented since some time the Prussian

fou de joie, se mit à danser, à danser
mad of joy himself set to dance to dance
    with   started

éperdument, en levant les bras et les jambes, à
passionately in raising the arms and the legs to
            while

danser en poussant des cris frénétiques, jusqu'au
dance in pushing -of the- cries frantic until the

moment où il tomba, épuisé au pied d'un
moment where he fell exhausted at the foot of a
base

mur.
wall

Il était prisonnier! Sauvé!
He was prisoner Saved

C'est ainsi que le château de Champignet fut
It is thus that the castle of Champignet was

repris à l'ennemi après six heures seulement
retaken at the enemy after six hours only
from

d'occupation.
of occupation

Le colonel Ratier, marchand de drap, qui enleva
The colonel Ratier merchant of cloth who executed

cette affaire à la tête des gardes nationaux de
this business at the head of the guards national of

la Roche-Oysel, fut décoré.
la   Roche-Oysel   was decorated

Un drame au bord de la mer I
A drama at the edge of the sea I

Balzac-- Un drame au bord de la mer I
Balzac A drama at the edge of the sea I

Les jeunes gens ont presque tous un compas
-The- Young people have almost all a compass

avec lequel ils se plaisent à mesurer
with which they -themselves- like to measure

l'avenir; quand leur volonté s'accorde avec la
the future when their will agrees with the

hardiesse de l'angle qu'ils ouvrent, le monde est
breadth of the angle that they open the world is

à eux. Mais ce phénomène de la vie morale
to them But this phenomenon of -the- life moral
theirs of inner values

n'a lieu qu'à un certain âge. Cet âge, qui,
not has place then to a certain age This age which
until

pour tous les hommes, se trouve entre
for all -the- men themselves find between
can be found

vingt-deux   et   vingt-huit   ans,   est   celui   des
twenty-two   and   twenty-eight   years   is   that   of the

grandes   pensées,   l'âge   des   conceptions
large   thoughts   the age   of the   concepts

premières,   parce   qu'il   est   l'âge   des   immenses
first   because   it   is   the age   of the   immense

désirs,   l'âge   où   l'on   ne   doute   de   rien: qui
desires   the age   where   one   -not-   doubts   -of-   nothing   who

dit   doute,   dit   impuissance.   Après   cet   âge   rapide
says   doubt   says   impotence   After   this   age   rapid

comme   une   semaison,   vient   celui   de   l'exécution.
like   a   sowing time   comes   that   of   the execution
                                                    execution

Il   est   en   quelque   sorte   deux   jeunesses,   la
It   is   in   some   way   two   youths   the
are

jeunesse   durant   laquelle   on   croit,   la   jeunesse
youth   during   which   one   believes   the   youth

pendant   laquelle   on   agit;   souvent   elles   se
during   which   one   acts   often   they

confondent chez les hommes que la nature a
confuse with the men that the nature has

favorisés, et qui sont, comme César, Newton et
favored and who are like Caesar Newton and

Bonaparte, les plus grands parmi les grands
Bonaparte the most great among the large

hommes. Je mesurais ce qu'une pensée veut de
men I measured this that a thought wants of
needs

temps pour se développer; et, mon compas à la
time -for- itself develop and my compass in the
to develop

main, debout sur un rocher, à cent toises
hand upright on a rock -with- hundred fathoms

au-dessus de l'Océan, dont les lames
above -of- the ocean of which the waves

se jouaient dans les brisants, j'arpentais mon
themselves played in the reefs I surveyed my
broke upon

avenir en le meublant d'ouvrages, comme un
future in it furnishing with works like an
while books

ingénieur qui, sur un terrain vide, trace des
engineer who on a ground empty traces -of the-

forteresses et des palais.
fortresses and -of the- palaces

La mer était belle, je venais de m'habiller après
The sea was beautiful I came of to dress me after
I just dressed myself

avoir nagé.
to have swum

J'attendais Pauline, mon ange gardien, qui se
I awaited Pauline my angel guardian who herself
guardian angel

baignait dans une cuve granit pleine d'un sable fin,
bathed in a cove granite full of a sand fine

la plus coquette baignoire que la nature ait
the most vain bath-tub that -the- nature has

dessinée pour ses fées marines.
designed for its fairies of the sea

Nous étions à l'extrémité du Croisic, une
We were at the extreme end of the Croisic a

mignonne presqu'île de la Bretagne; nous étions
nice peninsula of -the- Brittany we were

loin du port, dans un endroit que le
far from the port in a place that the

fisc a jugé tellement inabordable, que le
tax department has judged so much inaccessible that the

douanier n'y passe presque jamais.
customs officer not there passes almost never
tax officer there

Nager dans les airs après avoir nagé dans la
To swim in the air after to have swum in the
To float

mer! ah! qui n'aurait nagé dans l'avenir?
sea ah who would not have swum in the future

Pourquoi pensais-je? pourquoi vient un mal? qui le
Why thought I why comes an evil who it

sait? Les idées vous tombent au coeur ou à la
knows The ideas you fall on the heart or on the

tête sans vous consulter. Nulle courtisane ne
head without you to consult No courtisan -not-

fut plus fantasque ni plus impérieuse que ne
was more odd nor more pressing than -not-

l'est la conception pour les artistes; il faut la
it is the concept for the artists it is necessary it
is

prendre comme la fortune, à pleins cheveux,
to take like the fortune by full hair

quand elle vient. Grimpé sur ma pensée comme
when she comes Astride on my thought like
thoughts

Astolphe sur son hippogriffe, je
Astolphe on his hippogriff I
{fable creature half horse half eagle}

chevauchais donc à travers le monde, en y
galloped thus to through the world in there
while

disposant de tout à mon gré.
laying out of all with my liking
of

Quand je voulus chercher autour de moi quelque
When I wanted to search around -of- me some

présage pour les audacieuses constructions que ma
omen for the daring constructs that my
of

folle imagination me conseillait d'entreprendre, un
insane imagination me advised of to undertake a
to undertake

joli cri, le cri d'une femme qui sort d'un bain,
pretty cry the cry of a woman who leaves of a bath
a

ranimée, joyeuse, domina le murmure des
revived merry dominated the murmur of the

franges incessamment mobiles que dessinaient le
fringes incessantly mobile that drew the

flux et le reflux sur les découpures de la côte.
flux and the reflux on the cut outs of the coast

En entendant cette note jaillie de l'âme, je crus
In hearing this note gushed from the soul I believe
Hearing

avoir vu dans les rochers le pied d'un ange qui,
to have seen in the rocks the foot of an angel who

déployant ses ailes, s'était écrié: "Tu réussiras!" Je
deploying its wings was cried You will succeed I
had

descendis, radieux, léger; je descendis
descended radiant light I descended
lighthearted

en bondissant comme un caillou jeté sur une
in leaping as a pebble thrown on a
leaping off

pente rapide.
slope rapid

Quand elle me vit, elle me dit: "Qu'as-tu?"
When she me saw she me said What have you

Je ne répondis pas, mes yeux
I -not- answered not my eyes

se mouillèrent. La veille, Pauline avait
themselves became moist The night before Pauline had
became moist

compris mes douleurs, comme elle comprenait en
understood my pains like she understood in

ce moment mes joies, avec la sensibilité magique
this moment my joys with the sensitivity magic

d'une harpe qui obéit aux variations de
of a harp who obeys at the variations of

l'atmosphère.
the atmosphere

La vie humaine a de beaux moments!
The life human has -of- beautiful moments

Nous allâmes en silence le long des grèves.
We went in silence the length of the cliffs

Le ciel était sans nuages, la mer était sans
The sky was without clouds the sea was without

rides; d'autres n'y eussent vu que deux
ripples of others not there had seen that two
but

steppes bleus l'un sur l'autre; mais nous,
expanses blue the one on top of the other but we

nous qui nous entendions sans avoir besoin de
we who us understood without to have need of

la parole, nous qui pouvions faire jouer entre
the word we who could make to play between

ces deux langes de l'infini les illusions avec
these two layers of the infinite the illusions with

lesquelles on se repaît au jeune âge, nous
which one oneself nourishes at the young age we
himself nourishes

nous serrions la main au moindre changement
we gripped the hand at the least change

que présentaient, soit la nappe d'eau, soit les
that presented be it the sheet of water be it the
presented itself

nappes de l'air, car nous prenions ces légers
sheets of the sky because we took these light

phénomènes pour des traductions matérielles de
phenomena for -of the- translations material of

notre double pensée.
our double thought

Qui n'a pas savouré dans les plaisirs ce
Who not has not enjoyed in the pleasures that
has

moment de joie illimitée où l'âme semble s'être
moment of joy unlimited where the soul seems to be

débarrassée des liens de la chair, et se trouver
freed of the bonds of the flesh and itself find

comme rendue au monde d'où elle vient?
like returned to the world from where it comes

Le   plaisir   n'est   pas   notre   seul   guide   en   ces
The   pleasure is not   -not- our   only   guide   in   these

régions.
areas

N'est-il   pas   des   heures   où   les   sentiments
Is it not   not   of the   hours   where   the   feelings

s'enlacent   d'eux-mêmes   et   s'y   élancent,
intertwine   of themselves and and   themselves there hurl

comme   souvent   deux   enfants   se   prennent
like   often   two   children   each other   take

par   la   main   et   se   mettent   à   courir   sans
by   the   hand   and   themselves   put   to   run   without
                                        start

savoir   pourquoi?
to know   why

Nous   allions   ainsi.
We   went   like that

Au   moment   où   les   toits   de   la   ville   apparurent
At the   moment   where   the   roofs   of   the town   appeared

à l'horizon en y traçant une ligne grisâtre,
on the horizon in there tracing a line faint gray

nous rencontrâmes un pauvre pêcheur qui
we met a poor fisherman who

retournait au Croisic; ses pieds étaient nus, son
returned to the Croisic his feet were bare his
to

pantalon de toile était déchiqueté par le bas,
trousers of linen was shredded at the bottom
were

troué, mal raccommodé: puis, il avait une
perforated badly mended then he had a

chemise de toile à voile, de mauvaises bretelles
shirt of cloth for sail of bad straps
sails with

en lisière, et pour veste un haillon. Cette misère
in edge and for jacket a rag This misery
on edge

nous fit mal, comme si c'eût été quelque
us made badly like if there had been some

dissonance au milieu de nos harmonies. Nous
dissonance -at the- middle -of- our harmonies We
amid harmony

nous regardâmes **pour** nous **plaindre** **l'un**
us looked at for us to feel sorry for the one
each other

à l'autre **de** ne **pas** avoir **en** ce **moment** le
with the other of -not- not to have on this moment the

pouvoir de **puiser** dans **les** trésors **d'Aboul-Casem.**
ability of to draw in the treasures of Aboul Casem

Nous aperçûmes **un** superbe **homard** et **une**
We saw a superb lobster and a

araignée de **mer** accrochés **à** une **cordelette** que
spider of sea hung at a cord that
crab off

le pêcheur **balançait** dans **sa** main **droite,**
the fisherman balanced in its hand right

tandis que **de** l'autre **il** maintenait **ses** agrès **et**
while that off the other he held his tackle and
while

ses engins.
his machines

Nous l'accostâmes, **dans** l'intention **de** lui **acheter**
We accosted him in the intention of him to buy

sa pêche, idée qui nous vint à tous deux et qui
his fish idea that us came to all two and which
both

s'exprima dans un sourire auquel je répondis par
was expressed in a smile to which I answered with

une légère pression du bras que je tenais et
a light pressure on the arm that I held and

que je ramenai près de mon coeur.
that I brought back close of my heart
near

C'est de ces riens dont plus tard le souvenir
It is of these nothings of which more late the memory
later

fait des poèmes, quand auprès du feu nous
makes -of the- poems when close -of the- fire we

nous rappelons l'heure où ce rien nous a
us remember the hour where this nothing us has

émus, le lieu où ce fut, et ce mirage dont
moved the place where this was and this mirage of which
touched

les effets n'ont pas encore été constatés, mais
the effects do not have -not- yet been noted but

qui   s'exerce   souvent sur les objets qui nous
who   themselves exert   often   on   the   objects   who   us

entourent dans les moments où la vie est
surround   in   the   moments   where   the   life   is

légère et où nos coeurs sont pleins. Les sites
light   and where our   hearts   are   full   The   sites

les plus beaux ne sont que ce que nous les
the   most beautiful   not   are   but   that   what   we   them

faisons. Quel homme un peu poète n'a dans ses
make   Which   man   a   little   poet   not has   in   his

souvenirs un quartier de roche qui tient plus de
memories   a   quarter   of   rock   which   holds   more   -of-

place que n'en ont pris les plus célèbres
place   than   -not- there   have   taken   -the-   most   famous

aspects de pays cherchés à grands frais!
aspects   of countries   sought   at   large   costs

Près de ce rocher, de tumultueuses pensées; là,
Near   -of- that   rock   of   tumultuous   thoughts   there

toute une vie employée; là, des craintes
all a life employed there -of the- fears
evolved

dissipées; là, des rayons d'espérance sont
dispersed there of the rays of hope are
the have

descendus dans l'âme.
descended in the soul

En ce moment, le soleil, sympathisant avec ces
In this moment the sun sympathizing with these

pensées d'amour ou d'avenir, a jeté sur les
thoughts of love or of future has cast upon the

flancs fauves de cette roche une lueur ardente;
flancs savage of this rock a gleam burning

quelques fleurs des montagnes attiraient
some flowers of the mountains attracted

l'attention; le calme et le silence grandissaient
the attention the calm and the silence grew

cette anfractuosité sombre en réalité, colorée par
this ruggedness sombre in reality coloured by

le rêveur; alors elle était belle avec ses maigres
the dreamer then it was beautiful with its thin

végétations, ses camomilles chaudes, ses
vegetations its camomiles warm its

cheveux de Vénus aux feuilles veloutées.
hairs of Venus with leaves velvety
Love-in-a-mist flowers

Fête prolongée, décorations magnifiques,
Celebration prolonged decorations splendid

heureuse exaltation des forces humaines! Une fois
happy exaltation of the forces human One time

déjà le lac de Bienne, vu de l'île
already the lake of Bienne seen from the island

Saint-Pierre, m'avait ainsi parlé; le rocher du
Saint-Pierre had me thus spoken the rock of the
of

Croisic sera peut-être la dernière de ces joies.
Croisic will be perhaps the last of these joys

Mais alors, que deviendra Pauline?
But then what will become Pauline

"Vous avez fait une belle pêche ce matin, mon
You have made a beautiful fishing this morning my
catch

brave homme? dis-je au pêcheur."
dear man said I to the fisherman

"Oui, monsieur," répondit-il en s'arrêtant et en
Yes sir answered he in himself stopping and in
halting while

nous montrant la figure bistrée des gens qui
us showing the appearance darkened of the people who

restent pendant des heures entières exposés à
remain during -of the- hours whole exposed to

la réverbération du soleil sur l'eau.
the reflection of the sun on the water

Ce visage annonçait une longue résignation, la
This face announced a long resignation the

patience du pêcheur et ses moeurs douces. Cet
patience of the fisherman and his manners soft This

homme avait une voix sans rudesse, des lèvres
man had a voice without roughness -of the- lips

bonnes, nulle ambition, je ne sais quoi de grêle,
kind no ambition I not know what of frailty

de chétif. Toute autre physionomie nous aurait
of weakness All other aspect us would have

déplu.
displeased

"Où allez-vous vendre ça?"
Where are you going to sell that

"A la ville."
To the town

"Combien vous payera-t-on le homard?"
How much to you they will pay for the lobster

"Quinze sous."
Fifteen nickels

"L'araignée?"
The spider
The crab

"Vingt sous."
Twenty nickels

"Pourquoi tant de différence entre le homard
Why so much -of- difference between the lobster

et l'araignée?"
and the spider
the crab

"Monsieur, l'araignée (il la nommait 'iraigne') est
Sir the spider he it named iraigne is
the crab {in dialect}

bien plus délicate! puis, elle est maligne comme un
well more delicate then it is sly like a
and

singe, et se laisse rarement prendre."
monkey and itself lets seldom take

"Voulez-vous nous donner le tout pour cent
Want you us to give it all for hundred

sous?" dit Pauline.
nickels said Pauline

L'homme resta pétrifié.
The man remained petrified

"Vous ne l'aurez pas!" dis-je en riant, "j'en
You not will have it not said I in laughing I for it
while

donne   dix   francs.   Il   faut   savoir   payer   les
give   ten   franks   It   is necessary   to know   to pay   the

émotions   ce   qu'elles   valent."
emotions   this   that they   are worth

"Eh   bien,"   répondit-elle,   "je   l'aurai!   j'en   donne
Eh   well   - answered she   I   will have it   I for it   give

dix   francs   deux   sous."
ten   franks   two   nickels

"Dix   sous."
Ten   nickels

"Douze   francs."
Twelve   franks

"Quinze   francs."
Fifteen   franks

"Quinze   francs   cinquante   centimes,"   dit-elle.
Fifteen   franks   fifty   centimes   said she

"Cent   francs."
Hundred   franks

"Cent   cinquante."
Hundred   fifty

Je   m'inclinai.   Nous n'étions pas en   ce   moment
I   inclined myself We   were not -not- in   this   moment
     bowed

assez riches pour pousser plus haut cette enchère.
enough   rich   for   to push   more high   this   bidding

Notre pauvre pêcheur   ne   savait pas s'il devait
Our   poor   fisherman -not- knew   not if he   had

se   fâcher d'une mystification ou   se   livrer
himself to annoy of a   mystification   or   himself to deliver

à   la   joie; nous le   tirâmes de   peine en lui
to   -the- joy   we   him   drew   from pain   in him
                        freed   quandary

donnant le   nom   de notre hôtesse, et   en lui
giving   the name   of   our   hostess   and in him

recommandant de porter chez elle le homard et
recommending   of to carry with her the lobster and
                        to

l'araignée.
 the spider
the crab

"Gagnez-vous votre vie?" lui demandai-je, pour
Earn you your living him asked I for

savoir à quelle cause devait être attribué son
to know to which cause had to be allotted his

dénûment.
being bereft

"Avec bien de la peine et en souffrant bien des
With well of the pains and in suffering well of the

misères," me dit-il.
miseries me said he

"La pêche au bord de la mer, quand on n'a
The fish at the edge of the sea when one not has

ni barque ni filets, et qu'on ne peut la faire
nor boat nor nets and that one not can it do

qu'aux engins ou à la ligne, est un chanceux
but with the devices or with the line is a chance
rods

métier."
trade

"Voyez-vous, il faut y attendre le poisson
See it is necessary there to await the fish
(Understand) you

ou le coquillage, tandis que les grands pêcheurs
or the shell while that the large fishermen
while

vont le chercher en pleine mer. Il est si difficile
go it to seek in full sea It is so difficult

de gagner sa vie ainsi, que je suis le seul qui
of to earn ones life like this that I am the only who

pêche à la côte."
fishes at the coast

"Je passe des journées entières sans rien
I pass -of the- days whole without nothing

rapporter. Pour attraper quelque chose, il faut
to bring back For to catch some thing it is necessary
something

qu'une iraigne se soit oubliée à dormir comme
that an iraigne itself was forgotten to sleep like
{in dialect} had

celle-ci, ou qu'un homard soit assez
this-one or that a lobster should be enough

71

étourdi pour rester dans les rochers. Quelquefois
dazed for to remain in the rocks Sometimes

il y vient des lubines après la haute mer,
-it- there come -of the- bass after the high sea

alors je les empoigne."
then I them seize

"Enfin, l'un portant l'autre, que gagnez-vous par
Finally the one carrying the other what earn you per
added together

jour?"
day

"Onze à douze sous. Je m'en tirerais, si
Eleven to twelve nickels I myself of it would pull out if

j'étais seul, mais j'ai mon père à nourrir, et le
I was alone but I have my father to nourish and the

bonhomme ne peut pas m'aider, il est aveugle."
good man -not- can not help me he is blind

A cette phrase, prononcée simplement, nous nous
At this phrase pronounced simply we us

regardâmes, Pauline et moi, sans mot dire.
looked at   Pauline and me   without word to say
                                     a word

"Vous avez une femme ou quelque bonne amie?"
You   have   a woman or   some   good girlfriend

Il nous jeta l'un des plus déplorables regards
He us threw the one of the most deplorable looks
              one

que j'aie vus, en répondant:
that I have seen in   answering

"Si j'avais une femme, il   faudrait   donc
If   I had   a woman it would be necessary thus

abandonner mon père; je ne pourrais pas le
to give up   my father I -not- could not him

nourrir et nourrir encore une femme et des
nourish and nourish also a woman and -of the-

enfants."
children

"Eh bien! mon pauvre garçon, comment ne
Eh well my poor boy   how   not
                                why

cherchez-vous pas à gagner davantage en portant
seek you — not to gain more in carrying / by

du sel sur le port ou en travaillant aux
-of the- salt on / to the port or in working at the

marais salants?"
marsh salt / salt marshes

"Ah! monsieur, je ne ferais pas ce métier
Ah sir I not would make -not- this profession

pendant trois mois. Je ne suis pas assez fort,
during / more than three month I -not- am not enough strong

et si je mourais, mon père
and if I died my father

serait à la mendicité. Il me fallait un
would be to the begging / would be reduced to begging It (to) me was necessary a

métier qui ne voulût qu'un peu d'adresse et
trade that not wanted but a little of art and

beaucoup de patience."
much of patience

"Eh comment deux personnes peuvent-elles vivre
Eh   how   two   people   can they   live

avec douze sous par jour?"
with   twelve   nickels   per   day

"Oh! monsieur, nous mangeons des galettes de
Oh   sir   we   eat   -of the-   wafers   of

sarrasin et des bernicles que je détache des
buckwheat   and   -of the-   barnacles   that   I   detach   from the

rochers."
rocks

"Quel âge avez-vous donc?"
Which   age   have you   then

"Trente-sept ans."
Thirtyseven   years

"Êtes-vous sorti d'ici?"
Are you   gone out   from here
Have you

"Je suis allé une fois à Guérande pour tirer à
I   am   gone   one   time   with   Guérande   for   to draw   into
have

la milice, et suis allé à Savenay pour me faire
the militia and am gone to Savenay for me to let

voir à des messieurs qui m'ont mesuré. Si j'avais
see to of the gentlemen who have me measured If I had
of

eu un pouce de plus, j'étais soldat."
had one inch -of- more I was soldier

"Je serais crevé à la première fatigue, et mon
I would be done in at the first exhaustion and my

pauvre père demanderait aujourd'hui la charité."
poor father would ask today the charity

J'avais bien pensé des drames; Pauline était
I had well thought of the dramas Pauline was

habituée à de grandes émotions, près d'un
accustomed to -of- large emotions near of a

homme souffrant comme je le suis; eh bien!
man suffering like I it am eh well

jamais, ni l'un ni l'autre, nous n'avions
never nor the one nor the other us did not have

entendu de paroles plus émouvantes que ne
heard -of- words more moving touching that not

l'étaient celles de ce pêcheur. Nous fîmes quelques
it were those of this fisherman We made some

pas en silence, mesurant tous deux la profondeur
steps in silence measuring all both two the depth

muette de cette vie inconnue, admirant la
silent of this life unknown admiring the

noblesse de ce dévouement qui s'ignorait
nobility of this devotion which was unaware of

lui-même;
himself

la force de cette faiblesse nous étonna; cette
the force of this weakness us astonished this

insoucieuse générosité nous rapetissa. Je voyais ce
heedless generosity us reduced I saw this

pauvre être tout instinctif rivé sur ce rocher
poor being totally instinctive riveted chained on this rock

comme un galérien l'est à son boulet, y
like a galley slave it is/is to his ball (and chain) and

guettant depuis vingt ans des coquillages pour
watching for since twenty years of the/of shells to

gagner sa vie, et soutenu dans sa patience par
earn his living and supported in his patience by

un seul sentiment. Combien d'heures consumées
a single sentiment How many hours consumed/wasted

au coin d'une grève! Combien d'espérances
at the corner of a shore How much hopes

renversées par un grain, par un changement de
reversed by a grain by a change of

temps!
weather

il restait suspendu au bord d'une table de
he remained suspended/hanging from the edge of a slab of

granit, le bras tendu comme celui d'un faquir de
granite the arms extended like that of a fakir of

l'Inde, tandis que son père, assis sur une escabelle,
India while that his father sat on a stool
while

attendait, dans le silence et les ténèbres, le
waited in -the- silence and -the- darkness the

plus grossier des coquillages, et du pain, si le
more coarse of the shells and of the bread if it

voulait la mer.
wished the sea
permitted

"Buvez-vous quelquefois du vin?" lui demandai-je.
Drink you sometimes of the wine him asked I

"Trois ou quatre fois par an."
Three or four times per year

"Eh bien! vous en boirez aujourd'hui, vous et
Eh well you of it will drink today you and

votre père, et nous vous enverrons un pain
your father and we you will send a bread

blanc."
white

79

"Vous êtes bien bon, monsieur."
You   are   good good   sir
            noble

"Nous vous donnerons à dîner si vous voulez nous
We   you will give to dine if you want   us

conduire par le bord de la mer jusqu'à Batz,
to lead by   the edge of the sea until   Batz

où   nous irons   voir   la tour qui domine   le
where we   will go to see the tower that dominates the

bassin et les côtes entre   Batz et le Croisic."
basin and the coasts between Batz and the   Croisic

"Avec plaisir," nous dit-il.
With pleasure   us   said he

"Allez droit   devant   vous, en suivant   le chemin
Go   right   in front of you   in following the way
                                     following

dans lequel vous êtes, je vous y   retrouverai
in   which you are   I you there will find
on

après m'être   débarrassé   de mes agrès et de
after myself to be disencumbered of my tackle and of
       having myself gotten rid

ma pêche."
my   fish

Nous fîmes un même signe de consentement, et
We   made   a   same   sign   of   assent   and

il s'élança joyeusement vers la ville.
he   sprang   joyfully   towards the town

Cette rencontre nous maintint dans la situation
This   meeting   us   maintained   in   the condition

morale où nous étions, mais elle en avait
mental where we   were   but   she   of it had
                          had been   of it had

affaibli la gaieté.
weakened the cheerfulness

"Pauvre homme," me dit Pauline avec cet accent
Poor   man   to me said Pauline with this   tone

qui ôte à la compassion d'une femme ce
which removes to the compassion of a   woman this
              of

que la pitié peut avoir de blessant, "n'a-t-on pas
that the pity   can   have   of wounding   not had they not

honte   de   se   trouver heureux en voyant
shame   -of- themselves find   happy   in   seeing

cette misère?"
this   misery

"Rien   n'est plus cruel que d'avoir   des   désirs
Nothing is not more cruel than to have -of the- desires

impuissants," lui répondis-je.
impotent   her   answered I

"Ces deux pauvres êtres, le père et le fils, ne
These two   poor   beings the father and the son not

sauront pas plus combien ont été vives nos
will know -not- more how much have been keen   our

sympathies que le monde ne sait combien leur
sympathies   that the world not knows how much their

vie est belle,   car   ils amassent   des   trésors
life is beautiful because they   pile up   -of the- treasures

dans   le ciel."
in   -the- heaven

"Le pauvre pays!" dit-elle en me montrant le
The poor country said she in/while me showing the

long d'un champ environné d'un mur à pierres
length of a field surrounded by a wall with lumps

sèches, des bouses de vache appliquées
dry of the dungs of cow applied

symétriquement. J'ai demandé ce que c'était que
symmetrically I have asked this what it was but

cela. Une paysanne, occupée à les coller,
that A country-woman occupied with them to stick

m'a répondu qu'elle 'faisait du bois'.
me had answered that she made -of the- fuel

Imaginez-vous, mon ami, que, quand ces bouses
Imagine you my friend that when these dungs

sont séchées, ces pauvres gens les récoltent,
are dried these poor people them collect

les entassent et s'en chauffent.
them pile up and themselves of it heat

Pendant l'hiver, on les vend comme on vend
During the winter they them sell like one sells

des mottes de tan. Enfin, que crois-tu que gagne
of the mounds of peat Finally what believe you that earns

la couturière la plus chèrement payée? Cinq
the dressmaker the most dearly paid Five

sous par jour, dit-elle après une pause; mais on
nickels per day said she after a pause but they

la nourrit.
her feed

"Vois," lui dis-je, "les vents de mer dessèchent
See her said I the winds of (the) sea desiccate

ou renversent tout, il n'y a point
or bringing down everything it not there have any
                                    are

d'arbres; les débris des embarcations hors de
of trees the remains of the boats out of
trees

service se vendent aux riches, car le
service themselves sell to the rich because the
        are sold

prix des transports les empêche sans doute de
price of the transport them prevents without doubt of

consommer le bois de chauffage dont abonde
to consume the firewood of heating of which abounds

la Bretagne.
the Brittany

Ce pays n'est beau que pour les grandes ames;
This country is not fine but for the great souls

les gens sans coeur n'y vivraient pas; il ne
the people without heart not there would live -not- it not

peut être habité que par des poètes ou par
can be inhabited but by -of the- poets or by

des bernicles. N'a-t-il pas fallu que
-of the- barnacles Not has it not been necessary that
Wasn't it necessary

l'entrepôt du sel se plaçât sur ce rocher
the warehouse of the salt itself placed on this rock

pour qu'il fût habité? D'un côté, la mer; ici
for that it was inhabited Of one side the sea here

des   sables; en haut, l'espace."
of the   sands   in   high   the space

Un drame au bord de la mer II
A drama at the edge of the sea II

Balzac-- Un drame au bord de la mer II
Balzac   A   drama at the edge of the sea II

Nous avions déjà dépassé la ville, et nous
We   had   already passed the town and we

étions dans l'espèce de désert qui sépare le
were   in   the kind of desert that separates the

Croisic du bourg de Batz. Figurez-vous, mon
Croisic of the borough of Batz Imagine yourself my

cher oncle, une lande de deux lieues
dear uncle, a   barren track of land of two miles

remplie par le sable luisant qui se trouve au
filled   by the sand shining which itself finds at the

bord de la mer.
edge of the sea

Çà et là quelques rochers y levaient leurs
Here and there some   rocks there raised their

têtes, et vous eussiez dit des animaux
heads and you had said of the animals

gigantesques couchés dans les dunes. Le long de
gigantic asleep in the dunes The length of

la mer apparaissaient quelques récifs autour
the sea appeared some reefs around

desquels se jouait l'eau, en leur donnant
of which itself played water while them giving
     played

l'apparence de grandes roses blanches flottant sur
the appearance of large roses white floating on

l'étendue liquide et venant se poser sur le
the surface liquid and coming itself pose on the
     to pose itself

rivage. En voyant cette savane terminée par
shore In seeing this savanna ended at
     Seeing

l'Océan sur la droite, bordée sur la gauche
the Ocean on the right-hand side boarded on the left

par le grand lac que fait l'irruption de la mer
by the large lake that made the arm of the sea

entre le Croisic et les hauteurs sablonneuses de
between the Croisic and the heights sandy of

Guérande, au bas desquelles se trouvent
Guérande at the base of which themselves found
are found

des marais salants dénués de végétation,
of the marshes salts stripped of vegetation
the salt marshes

je regardai Pauline en lui demandant si elle
I looked at Pauline in her asking if she

se sentait le courage d'affronter les ardeurs
themselves felt the courage to face the ardor
felt

du soleil et la force de marcher dans le
of the sun and the strength of to walk in the
walking

sable.
sand

"J'ai des brodequins, allons-y," me dit-elle en
I have -of the- laced boots let us go there me said she while

me montrant la tour de Batz qui arrêtait la
me showing the tower of Batz which halted the

vue par une construction placée là comme une
sight by a construction placed there like a
with

pyramide, mais une pyramide fuselée, découpée,
pyramid but a pyramid tapered cut out
slender outlined

une pyramide si poétiquement ornée, qu'elle
a pyramid so poetically decorated that it

permettait à l'imagination d'y voir la
allowed -at- the imagination of there to see the

première des ruines d'une grande ville asiatique.
first of the ruins of a large city Asian

Nous fîmes quelques pas pour aller nous asseoir
We made some steps for to go ourselves seat

sur la portion d'une roche qui se trouvait
on the part of a rock that itself found

encore ombrée;
still shaded

mais il était onze heures du matin, et cette
but it was eleven hours of the morning and this
in the

ombre, qui cessait à nos pieds, s'effaçait
shade which stopped at our feet was disappearing

avec rapidité. "Combien ce silence est beau," me
with speed How this silence is beautiful me
rapidly

dit-elle,
said she

"et comme la profondeur en est étendue par le
and how the depth of it is extended by the

retour égal du frémissement de la mer sur
return equal -of the- quiver of the sea on
rhythmic

cette plage."
this beach

"Si tu veux livrer ton entendement aux trois
If you want to deliver your mind to the three

immensités qui nous entourent, l'eau, l'air et
vastnesses which us surround the water the air and

les sables, en écoutant exclusivement le son
the sands in listening exclusively (to) the sound

répété   du   flux   et   du   reflux,"   lui
repeated   of the   flow   and   of the   backward flow   her

répondis-je, "tu   n'en   supporteras   pas   le   langage,
answered I   you   not of it   will support   -not-   the   language

tu   croiras   y   découvrir   une   pensée   qui
you   will believe   there   to discover   a   thought   which

t'accablera.   Hier,   au   coucher   du   soleil,
will weigh you down / overwhelm you   Yesterday   at the   setting   of the   sun

j'ai   eu   cette   sensation;   elle   m'a   brisé."
I have   had   this   feeling   it   me has   broken

"Oh!   oui,   parlons,"   dit-elle   après   une   longue   pause.
Oh   yes   let us speak   said she   after   a   long   pause

"Aucun   orateur   n'est   plus   terrible.   Je   crois
No   speaker   is not   more   terrible   I   believe

découvrir   les   causes   des   harmonies   qui   nous
to discover   the   causes   of the   harmony   which   us

environnent,"   reprit-elle.
surround   began again she

"Ce paysage, qui n'a que trois couleurs
This landscape which not has that three colors
but

tranchées, le jaune brillant des sables, l'azur
cut neatly the yellow shining of the sands the azure

du ciel et le vert uni de la mer, est grand
of the sky and the green even of the sea is great

sans être sauvage, il est immense, sans être
without to be savage it is immense without to be

désert; il est monotone, sans être fatigant; il
desert it is monotonous without to be tiring it

n'a que trois éléments, il est varié."
not has that three elements (but) it is varied
but

"Les femmes seules savent rendre ainsi leurs
The women alone know to render thus their

impressions," répondis-je, "tu serais désespérante
impressions answered I you would be despairing

pour un poète, chère âme que j'ai si bien
for a poet dear soul that I have so well

devinée!"
divined

"L'excessive chaleur du midi jette à ces trois
The excessive heat of the midday cast at these three

expressions de l'infini une couleur dévorante,"
expressions of the infinite a color devouring

reprit Pauline en riant. "Je conçois ici les
began again Pauline in laughing I conceive here the
                        laughing

poésies et les passions de l'Orient."
poetries and the passions of the East

"Et moi, j'y conçois le désespoir."
And me I there conceive the despair

"Oui," dit-elle, "cette dune est un cloître sublime."
Yes said she this dune is a cloister sublime

Nous entendîmes le pas pressé de notre guide; il
We heard the steps hasty of our guide he

s'était endimanché. Nous lui
himself was in-Sunday-ed We him
himself had dressed up in his Sunday clothes

adressâmes quelques paroles insignifiantes; il
addressed some words unimportant he

crut voir que nos dispositions d'âme avaient
believed to see that our disposition of soul had
of the soul

changé; et, avec cette réserve que donne le
changed and with this reserve that gives the

malheur, il garda le silence.
misery he kept the silence

Quoique nous nous pressassions
Though we ourselves pressed

de temps en temps la main pour nous avertir
of time in time the hand for ourselves to inform
now and then

de la mutualité de nos idées et de nos
of the reciprocity of our ideas and of our

impressions, nous marchâmes pendant une
impressions we went during one

demi-heure en silence, soit que nous fussions
half hour in silence be it that we were

95

accablés par la chaleur qui s'élançait en
overpowered by the heat which launched itself in

ondées brillantes du milieu des sables, soit
waves brilliant from the middle of the sands (or) be it

que la difficulté de la marche employât notre
that the difficulty of the march employed our

attention.
attention

Nous allions en nous tenant par la main, comme
We went in us holding by the hand like

deux enfants; nous n'eussions pas fait douze pas
two children we -not had- not made twelve steps

si nous nous étions donné le bras.
if we us were given the arm
                    had go arm in arm

Le chemin qui mène au bourg de Batz n'était
The road which leads to the borough of Batz was not

pas tracé; il suffisait d'un coup de vent pour
-not- marked it was enough of one blow of wind for

effacer les marques que laissaient les pieds de
to erase the marks that left the feet of

chevaux ou les jantes de charrette; mais l'oeil
horses or the wheels of cart but the eye

exercé de notre guide reconnaissait à quelques
practiced of our guide recognized by some

fientes de bestiaux, à quelques parcelles de
droppings of cattle by some pieces of

crottin, ce chemin qui tantôt descendait vers
mud this way which sometimes went down towards

la mer, tantôt remontait vers les terres, au
the sea sometimes went up towards the grounds at the
landwards

gré des pentes, ou pour tourner des rochers.
liking of the slopes or for to go around of the rocks
of

A midi, nous n'étions qu'à mi-chemin.
At midday we were not but at half way

"Nous nous reposerons là-bas," dis-je
We ourselves will rest down there said I

en montrant le promontoire composé de rochers
in climbing the headland composed of rocks
  pointing to

assez élevés pour faire supposer que nous y
enough raised for to let assume that we there

trouverions une grotte.
should find a cave

En m'entendant, le pêcheur, qui avait suivi la
In hearing me the fisherman who had followed the

direction de mon doigt, hocha la tête, et me dit:
direction of my finger shook the head and me told

"Il y a là quelqu'un."
-It- there has there somebody
        is

"Ceux qui viennent du bourg de Batz au
Those who come of the borough of Batz to the

Croisic, ou du Croisic au bourg de Batz,
Croisic or from the Croisic to the borough of Batz

font tous un détour pour n'y point passer."
make all a detour for not there not to pass
                              there

Les paroles de cet homme furent dites à voix

The words of this man were said with voice

basse, et supposaient un mystère.

low and indicated a mystery

"Est-ce donc un voleur, un assassin?"

Is it thus a robber an assassin

Notre guide ne nous répondit que par une

Our guide not us answered but by an

aspiration creusée qui redoubla notre curiosité.

aspiration deep which redoubled our curiosity

"Mais, si nous y passons, nous arrivera-t-il

But if we there pass us will arrive it

quelque malheur?"

some misfortune

"Oh! non."

Oh no

"Y passerez-vous avec nous?"

There will pass you with us

"Non, monsieur."
No — sir

"Nous irons donc, si vous nous assurez qu'il
We will go thus if you us ensure that it

n'y a nul danger pour nous."
not there has no danger for us

"Je ne dis pas cela," répondit vivement le pêcheur.
I not say not that answered hastily the fisherman

"Je dis seulement que celui qui s'y trouve
I say only that that one who himself there finds

ne vous dira rien et ne vous fera aucun mal.
not you will say nothing and not you will do no harm

Oh! mon Dieu, il ne bougera seulement pas de sa
Oh my God he not will budge/will move only not of his

place."
place

"Qui est-ce donc?"
Who is this then

"Un homme!"
A   man

Jamais deux syllabes ne furent prononcées d'une
Never two syllables -not- were pronounced of a
in a

façon si tragique. En ce moment, nous étions à
way so tragically In this moment we were at

une vingtaine de pas de ce récif dans lequel
a score of steps of this reef in which

se jouait la mer; notre guide prit le chemin qui
itself played the sea our guide took the road that
played

entourait les rochers; nous continuâmes droit
went around the rocks we continued right

devant nous; mais Pauline me prit le bras.
in front of us but Pauline me took the arm

Notre guide hâta le pas, afin de se trouver
Our guide hastened the step so of himself to find

en même temp que nous à l'endroit où les
in (the) same time like us at the place where the

deux chemins se rejoignaient. Il supposait
two ways themselves joined He supposed
joined

sans doute qu'après avoir vu l'homme, nous
without doubt that after to have seen the man we

irions d'un pas pressé. Cette circonstance alluma
would go of a step pressed This circumstance lit

notre curiosité, qui devint alors si vive, que nos
our curiosity which became then so lively that our

coeurs palpitèrent comme si nous eussions
hearts beat as if we had

éprouvé un sentiment de peur.
experienced a feeling of fear

Malgré la chaleur du jour et l'espèce de
In spite of the heat of the day and the sort of

fatigue que nous causait la marche dans les
exhaustion that us caused the march in the

sables, nos âmes étaient encore livrées à la
sands our hearts were still delivered to the

mollesse indicible d'une merveilleuse extase;
softness inexpressible of a marvellous extasy

elles étaient pleines de ce plaisir pur qu'on ne
they were full of this pleasure pure that one not

saurait peindre qu'en le comparant à celui
would know to paint but in the comparing with that

qu'on ressent en écoutant quelque délicieuse
what one feels in listening some wonderful

musique, l'andiamo mio ben de Mozart.
music the we go my dear of Mozart
the 'andiamo mio ben'

Deux sentiments purs qui se confondent,
Two sentiments pure which themselves mix
intermingled

ne sont-ils pas comme deux belles voix qui
-not- are they not like two beautiful voices that

chantent?
sing

Pour pouvoir bien apprécier l'émotion qui vint
For to be able well to appreciate the emotion that came

nous saisir, il faut donc partager l'état à
us to seize it is necessary thus to divide the state -at-

demi voluptueux dans lequel nous avaient plongés
half sensuous in which we had plunged

les événements de cette matinée.
the events of this morning

Admirez pendant longtemps une tourterelle aux
Admire for a long time a turtle-dove with

jolies couleurs, posée sur un souple rameau, près
pretty colors posed on a flexible branch near

d'une source, vous jetterez un cri de douleur en
of a source you will throw a cry of pain in
utter

voyant tomber sur elle un émouchet qui lui
seeing to fall on it a goshawk that him

enfonce ses griffes d'acier jusqu'au coeur et
inserts its claws of steel right into the heart and

l'emporte avec la rapidité meurtrière que la
it carries with the speed deadly that the

poudre communique au boulet. Quand nous
(gun)powder communicates to the bullet When we

eûmes fait un pas dans l'espace qui se trouvait
had made a step in the space which itself found
                                                               was found

devant la grotte, espèce d'esplanade située à
in front of the cave sort of esplanade located at
                                           of an esplanade

cent pieds au-dessus de l'Océan, et défendue
hundred feet above -of- the ocean and defended

contre ses fureurs par une cascade de rochers
against its furies by a cascade of rocks

abruptes, nous éprouvâmes un frémissement
abrupt we experienced a slight shock

électrique assez semblable au sursaut que cause
electric enough similar at the start that causes

un bruit soudain au milieu d'une nuit silencieuse.
a noise sudden at the middle of a night quiet
                                       in the

Nous avions vu, sur un quartier de granit, un
We had seen on a mass of granite a

homme   assis   qui   nous   avait   regardés.   Son
man   sat   who   us   had   looked at   his
being seated

coup d'oeil,   semblable   à   la   flamme   d'un   canon,
strike of eye   similar   to   the   flame   of a   gun
glance

sortit   de   deux   yeux   ensanglantés,   et   son
came out   of   two   eyes   bloodshot   and   his

immobilité   stoïque   ne   pouvait   se   comparer
immobility   stoical   not   could   themselves   compare
be compared

qu'à   l'inaltérable   attitude   des   piles   granitiques
but with   the inalterable   attitude   of the   piles   granitic

qui   l'environnaient.   Ses   yeux   se   remuèrent
which   him surrounded   His   eyes   themselves   moved
moved

par   un   mouvement   lent,   son   corps   demeura   fixe,
with   a   movement   slow   his   body   remained   fixed

comme   s'il   eût   été   pétrifié;   puis,   après   nous   avoir
like   if it   had   been   petrified   then   after   us   to have

jeté   ce   regard   qui   nous   frappa   violemment,   il
cast   this   glance   that   us   struck   violently   he

reporta ses yeux sur l'étendue de l'Océan, et la
deferred his eyes on the extent of the Ocean and her

contempla malgré la lumière qui en jaillissait,
contemplated in spite of the light which of it sprayed

comme on dit que les aigles contemplent le
like one says that the eagles contemplate the
     would say

soleil, sans baisser ses paupières, qu'il ne releva
sun without to drop their eyelids that he not raised

plus.
more

Cherchez à vous rappeler, mon cher oncle, une de
Seek to -you- recall my dear uncle one of
Try

ces vieilles truisses de chêne, dont le
these old hedge branch bundles of oak of which the

tronc noueux, ébranché de la veille, s'élève
trunk gnarly pruned of the caretaker rises

fantastiquement sur un chemin désert, et vous
as in a fantasy on a road deserted and you

aurez une image vraie de cet homme. C'était des
will have an image true of this man It was of the

formes herculéennes ruinées, un visage de Jupiter
forms herculean ruined a face of Jupiter

Olympien, mais détruit par l'âge, par les rudes
Olympian but destroyed by the age by the hard

travaux de la mer, par le chagrin, par une
work of the sea by the sorrow by a

nourriture grossière, et comme noirci par un
food coarse and as if blackened by a

éclat de foudre.
strike of lightning

En voyant ses mains poilues et dures, j'aperçus
In seeing his hands hairy and hard I saw
  Seeing

 des nerfs qui ressemblaient à des veines de
-of the- tendons which resembled at of the veins of

fer. D'ailleurs, tout en lui dénotait une
iron Moreover everything in him indicated a

constitution vigoureuse.
constitution vigorous

Je remarquai dans un coin de la grotte une
I noted in a corner of the cave an

assez grande quantité de mousse, et sur une
enough large quantity of moss and on a

grossière tablette taillée par le hasard au
coarse shelf cut by -the- chance at the
                                        in the

milieu du granit, un pain rond cassé qui
middle of the granite a bread round broken which

couvrait une cruche de grès. Jamais mon
covered a jug of earthenware Never my

imagination, quand elle me reportait vers les
imagination when it me brought towards the

déserts où vécurent les premiers anachorètes de
deserts where lived the first anchorites of

la chrétienté, ne m'avait dessiné de figure plus
the christendom not had me drawn of appearance more

grandement religieuse ni plus horriblement
greatly religious nor more awfully

repentante que l'était celle de cet homme. Vous
repentant than it was that of this man You

qui avez pratiqué le confessionnal, mon cher
who have practised the confessional my dear

oncle, vous n'avez jamais peut-être vu un si
uncle you not have never maybe seen a so
have

beau remords, mais ce remords était noyé
beautiful remorse but this remorse was drowned

dans les ondes de la prière, la prière continue
in the waves of -the- prayer -the- prayer continuous

d'un muet désespoir.
of a dumb despair

Ce pêcheur, ce marin, ce Breton grossier était
This fisherman this sailor this Breton coarse was

sublime par un sentiment inconnu.
sublime by a feeling unknown

Mais ces yeux avaient-ils pleuré?
But these eyes had they cried

Cette main de statue ébauchée avait-elle frappé?
This hand of (a) statue outlined had it struck

Ce front rude, empreint de probité farouche, et
This face hard imbued of probity savage and

sur lequel la force avait néanmoins laissé les
on which the force had nevertheless left the

vestiges de cette douceur qui est l'apanage de
vestiges of this softness which is the prerogative of

toute force vraie, ce front sillonné de rides,
all force true this face furrowed of wrinkles

était-il en harmonie avec un grand coeur?
was it in harmony with a great heart

Pourquoi cet homme dans le granit? Pourquoi le
Why this man in the granite Why the

granit dans cet homme? Où était l'homme, où
granite in this man Where was the man where

111

était   le   granit?
was   the   granite

Il   nous   tomba   tout   un   monde   de   pensées   dans
It   (on) us   fell   all   a   world   of   thoughts   in
There   a whole world

la   tête.   Comme   l'avait   supposé   notre   guide,   nous
the   head   Like   it had   supposed   our   guide   we

passâmes   en   silence,   promptement,   et   il   nous
passed   in   silence   promptly   and   he   us

revit   émus   de   terreur   ou   saisis   d'étonnement,
saw again   moved   by   terror   or   seized   by astonishment

mais   il   ne   s'arma   point   contre   nous   de   la
but   he   not   himself armed   not at all   against   us   -of-   the
used

réalité   de   ses   prédictions.
reality   of   his   predictions

"Vous   l'avez   vu?"   dit-il.
You   him have   seen   said he

"Quel   est   cet   homme?"   dis-je.
What   is   this   man   said I

"On l'appelle l'Homme au voeu".
They call him the Man with the vow

Vous figurez-vous bien à ce mot le mouvement
You imagine yourself well at this word the movement

par lequel nos deux têtes se tournèrent
by which our two heads themselves turned

vers notre pêcheur! C'était un homme simple; il
towards our fisherman It was a man simple he

comprit notre muette interrogation, et voici ce
understood our silent interrogation and here this

qu'il nous dit dans son langage, auquel je tâche
what he us told in his language to which I try

de conserver son allure populaire.
of to preserve its pace popular

"Madame, ceux du Croisic, comme ceux de Batz,
Madam those of the Croisic like those of Batz

croient que cet homme est coupable de
believe that this man is guilty of

quelque chose, et fait une pénitence ordonnée
some thing and does a penitence ordered
something

par un fameux recteur auquel il est allé
by a famous vice-chancellor to which he is gone

se confesser plus loin que Nantes."
himself to confess more far than Nantes
farther

"D'autres croient que Cambremer, c'est son nom,
Others believe that Cambremer it is his name

a une mauvaise chance qu'il communique à
has a bad fortune that it communicates to

qui passe sous son air."
whomever pass under its air
influence

"Aussi plusieurs, avant de tourner sa roche,
Also several before of to turn around his rock

regardent-ils d'où vient le vent!"
look at they from where comes the wind

"S'il est de galerne, dit-il en nous montrant
If it is of northwesterly said he in us showing

l'ouest, ils ne continueraient pas leur chemin
the west they not would continue -not- their way

quand il s'agirait d'aller quérir un morceau
(even) when it would concern of going to gather a piece

de la vraie croix; ils retournent, ils ont peur."
of the true cross they turn back they have fear

"D'autres, les riches du Croisic, disent que
Others the rich of the Croisic say that

Cambremer a fait un voeu, d'où son nom
Cambremer has made a vow from where his name

l'Homme au voeu."
the Man with the vow

"Il est là nuit et jour, sans en sortir." "Ces
He is there night and day without in leaving These

dires ont une apparence de raison."
statements have an appearance of reason

"Voyez-vous," dit-il en se retournant pour nous
See you said he in himself turning for us

montrer une chose que nous n'avions pas
to show a thing that we did not have -not-

remarquée, "il a planté là, à gauche, une croix
noticed he has planted there at (the) left a cross

de bois pour annoncer qu'il s'est mis sous la
of wood for to announce that he himself is put under the
himself has

protection de Dieu, de la sainte Vierge et des
protection of God of the holy Virgin and of the

saints."
saints

"Il ne se serait pas sacré comme ça, que
He not himself would be not enthroned like that that
but for

la frayeur qu'il donne au monde fait qu'il est
the fright that he gives with world fact that he is

là en sûreté comme s'il était gardé par de la
there in safety like if he was kept by of the

troupe."
troop
troops

"Il n'a pas dit un mot depuis qu'il s'est
He not has not said one word since that he himself is
has himself has

enfermé en plein air; il se nourrit de pain et
locked up in open air he himself nourishes of bread and

d'eau que lui apporte tous les matins la fille
of water that him brings all the mornings the daughter

de son frère, une petite tronquette de douze ans,
of his brother a little lass of twelve years
girl

à laquelle il a laissé ses biens, et qu'est une
at which he has left his goods and that is a

jolie créature douce comme un agneau, une bien
pretty creature soft like a lamb a very

mignonne fille, bien plaisante. Elle vous a, dit-il
nice girl very kind She -you- has said he

en montrant son pouce, des yeux bleus longs
in showing his thumb -of the- eyes blue long
large

comme ça, sous une chevelure de chérubin."
like that under a hair of (a) cherub

"Quand on lui demande: 'Dis donc, Pérotte? (Ça
When one her asks Tell then Pérotte That
                  Tell me

veut dire chez nous Pierrette, fit-il en
wants to say with us Pierrette made he in

s'interrompant; elle est vouée à saint Pierre;
interrupting himself she is dedicated to saint Peter

Cambremer s'appelle Pierre, il a été son
Cambremer himself calls Pierre he has been her
                        Peter

parrain)."
godfather

"'Dis donc, Pérotte, reprit-il qué qui te dit
Tell then Pérotte began again he what that you says
Tell me   what is it

ton oncle?' 'Il ne me dit rin, qu'elle répond,
your uncle He not me says noth'n that she answers
                      nothing

rin du tout, rin.' 'Eh bien! qué qu'il te
noth'n of the all noth'n Eh well what that he you
nothing at nothing   what is it

fait?' 'Il m'embrasse au front le dimanche.' 'Tu
does He kisses me on the forehead the Sunday You

n'en   as   pas peur?' 'Ah ben!   qu'a   dit,   il
not of him have -not- fear   Ah   well that has (she) said he

est   mon   parrain.   Il   n'a pas voulu   d'autre
is   my   godfather He   has not wanted of other
                                                of any other

personne pour lui apporter à manger.'"
person   for him bring   to eat
            to

"Pérotte   prétend   qu'il   sourit   quand   elle   vient,
Pérotte   claims   that he smiles   when   she   comes

mais autant dire   un rayon de soleil dans la
but   as much to say a   ray   of sun   in   the

brouine,   car   on   dit   qu'il   est nuageux comme
mist   because one says that he is   cloudy   like

un brouillard."
a   fog

"Mais,"   lui   dis-je,   "vous excitez notre curiosité
But   him   said I   you   excite   our   curiosity

sans   la satisfaire.   Savez-vous   ce   qui   l'a
without it to satisfy   Do you know that that which him has

conduit là? Est-ce le chagrin? est-ce le
led · there · Is it · -the- · sorrow · is it · -the-

repentir? est-ce une manie? est-ce un crime?
repentance · is it · a · craze · is it · a · crime

est-ce..."
is it

"Eh, monsieur, il n'y a guère que
Eh · sir · it · not there · has · hardly (anyone) · (other) than

mon père et moi qui sachions la vérité de la
my · father · and · me · who · know · the · truth · of · the

chose."
thing

Un drame au bord de la mer III
A drama at the edge of the sea III

Balzac-- Un drame au bord de la mer III
Balzac   A   drama   at the   edge   of   the   sea   III

"Défunt ma mère servait un homme de justice à
Late   my   mother   served   a   man   of   justice   to

qui Cambremer a tout dit par ordre du
whom   Cambremer   has   all   told   by   order   of the

prêtre qui ne lui a donné l'absolution qu'à cette
priest   who   not   him   has   given   the absolution   but on   this

condition-là, à entendre les gens du port."
condition there   to   hear   the   people   of the   port

"Ma pauvre mère a entendu Cambremer sans le
My   poor   mother   has   heard   Cambremer   without   it

vouloir, parce que la cuisine du justicier
to want   by-this that   the   kitchen   of the   dispenser of justice
because

était à côté de sa salle; elle a
was   at   side   of   her   room   she   has

écouté! Elle est morte; le juge qu'a écouté est
heard She has died the judge that has listened is

défunt aussi. Ma mère nous a fait promettre,
passed away also My mother us has made to promise

à mon père et à moi, de n'en rin afférer
to my father and to me of not of it noth'n to relate
                              of it nothing to tell

aux gens du pays; mais je puis vous dire à
to the people of the country but I can -you- say to

vous que le soir où ma mère nous a
you that the evening where my mother us has
                        when

raconté ça, les cheveux me grésillaient dans la
told that the hair me turned gray in the
                                              on

tête."
head

"Eh bien, dis-nous ça, mon garçon, nous n'en
Eh well tell us that my boy we not of it
                                              of it

parlerons à personne."
will speak to no-one

Le pêcheur nous regarda, et continua ainsi:
The fisherman us looked at and continued as follows

"Pierre Cambremer, que vous avez vu là, est
Pierre Cambremer that you have seen there is

l'aîné des Cambremer, qui de père en fils sont
the elder of the Cambremer who of father in son are
the eldest

marins; leur nom le dit, la mer a toujours
sailors their name it means the sea has always

plié sous eux."
folded under them

"Celui que vous avez vu s'était fait pêcheur à
The one that you have seen was made fisherman at

bateaux. Il avait donc des barques, allait pêcher
boats He had thus of the boats went to fish

la sardine, il pêchait aussi le haut poisson, pour
the sardine he fished also the high fish for
big

les marchands."
the merchants

"Il aurait armé un bâtiment et pêché la
He would have armed a trawler and fished the
chartered

morue, s'il n'avait pas tant aimé sa femme,
cod if he did not have -not- so much loved his wife

qui était une belle femme, une Brouin de
who was a beautiful woman a Brouin of

Guérande, une fille superbe, et qui avait bon
Guérande a girl superb and who had (a) good

coeur."
heart

"Elle aimait tant Cambremer, qu'elle n'a jamais
She loved so much Cambremer that she not has never
so much loved

voulu que son homme la quittât plus du
wanted that her husband her left more than the

temps nécessaire à la pêche aux sardines."
time necessary at the fishing of the sardines

"Ils demeuraient là-bas, tenez!" dit le pêcheur
They remained down there behold said the fisherman
lived

en montant sur une éminence pour nous montrer
in climbing on a hillock for us to show
climbing

un îlot dans la petite méditerranée qui se
a small island in the small mediterranean that itself
middle sea

trouve entre les dunes où nous marchions et
finds between the dunes where we went and

les marais salants de Guérande, "voyez-vous cette
the marshes salt of Guérande see you this
salt marshes

maison? Elle était à lui. Jacquette Brouin et
house It was to him Jacquette Brouin and
of

Cambremer n'ont eu qu'un enfant, un garçon
Cambremer not have had but one child a boy

qu'ils ont aimé... comme quoi dirai-je? dame!
that they have loved like what will say I lady

comme on aime un enfant unique; ils en étaient
like one loves an child only they in it were
only child

fous."
insane

"Leur   petit   Jacques   aurait   fait,
Their   small   Jacques   would have   done
                                       done his necessities

sous votre respect,   dans   la   marmite   qu'ils
under your   respect   in   the   pot   that they
  with all due respect

auraient   trouvé   que   c'était   du   sucre."
would have   found   that   it was   of the   sugar
              thought

"Combien   donc   que   nous   les   avons   vus   de   fois,   à
How much   then   that   we   them   have   seen   of   time   at
                                                                    at   times

la   fore,   acheter   les   plus   belles   breloques   pour
the   fair   to buy   the   most   beautiful   charms   for
                                                      toys

lui!"
him

"C'était   de   la   déraison,   tout   le   monde   le   leur
It was   of   the   insanity   all   the   world   it   them
                        insane

disait."
said

"Le   petit   Cambremer,   voyant   que   tout   lui   était
The   small   Cambremer   seeing   that   all   him   was

permis, est devenu méchant comme un âne rouge."
permitted is become malicious like an ass red
    has   red ass

"Quand on venait dire au père Cambremer:
When one came to say to the father Cambremer

'Votre fils a manqué tuer le petit un tel!'
Your son has missed to kill the little one such-and-such
              almost killed

il riait et disait: 'Bah! ce sera un fier marin!
he laughed and said Bah this will be a proud sailor

il commandera les flottes du roi.' Un autre:
he will command the fleets of the king An other

'Pierre Cambremer, savez-vous que votre gars a
Pierre Cambremer know you that your boy has

crevé l'oeil de la petite Pougaud?' 'Il aimera les
poked the eye of the small girl Pougaud He will like the

filles!' disait Pierre. Il trouvait tout bon. Alors mon
girls said Pierre He found all good Then my

petit mâtin, à dix ans, battait tout le monde et
little cur at ten years fought all the world and

s'amusait à couper le cou aux poules, il
amused himself with to cut the neck of the hens he

éventrait les cochons, enfin il se roulait dans
ripped open the pigs in all he himself wallowed in

le sang comme une fouine. 'Ce sera un
the blood like a long pitchfork This will be a

fameux soldat!' disait Cambremer, 'il a goût au
famous soldier said Cambremer he has taste of the

sang.'"
blood

"Voyez-vous, moi, je me suis souvenu de tout ça,"
See you me I me am remembered of all that

dit le pêcheur. "Et Cambremer aussi," ajouta-t-il
said the fisherman And Cambremer also added he

après une pause. "A quinze ou seize ans, Jacques
after a pause At fifteen or sixteen years Jacques

Cambremer était... quoi? un requin."
Cambremer was what a shark

"Il allait s'amuser à Guérande, ou faire le joli
He went to have fun at Guérande or to make the pretty

coeur à Savenay. Fallait des espèces."
heart at Savenay Needed -of the- expenses

"Alors il se mit à voler sa mère, qui
Then he himself put to steal his mother who
began steal from

n'osait en rien dire à son mari. Cambremer
did not dare of it nothing to say to her husband Cambremer

était un homme probe à faire vingt lieues
was a man honest (enough) to make twenty miles

pour rendre à quelqu'un deux sous qu'on lui
for to return to somebody two nickels that one him

aurait donné de trop dans un compte."
would have given of too much in an account

"Enfin, un jour la mère fut dépouillée de tout."
Finally one day the mother was stripped of everything

"Pendant une pêche de son père, le fils
During a fishing trip of his father the kid

emporta le buffet, la mette, les draps, le
carried the buffet the settings the cloths the
pots and pans

linge, ne laissa que les quatre murs, il avait
linen not left but the four walls he had

tout vendu pour aller faire ses frigousses à
everything sold for to go to make his capers at

Nantes. La pauvre femme en a pleuré pendant
Nantes The poor woman of it has cried during

des jours et des nuits."
-of the- days and -of the- nights

"Fallait dire ça au père à son retour, elle
Was necessary to tell that to the father at his return she

craignait le père, pas pour elle, allez! Quand
feared the father not for herself go When
you know

Pierre Cambremer revint, qu'il vit sa maison
Pierre Cambremer returned that he saw his house

garnie   des   meubles   que   l'on   avait
furnished   of the   pieces of furniture   that   to her they   had
          with the

prêtés   à   sa   femme,   il   dit:
borrowed   to   his   wife   he   said

'Qu'est-ce que c'est que ça?'"
What is   that   it is   that   that
    What is it

"La   pauvre   femme   était   plus   morte   que   vive,   elle
The   poor   woman   was   more   dead   than   alive   she

dit: 'Nous   avons   été   volés.'   'Où   donc   est
said   We   have   been   robbed   Where   then   is

Jacques?' Jacques,   il   est   en   riole!'"
Jacques   Jacques   he   is   in   debauchery
              amusing oneself

"Personne   ne   savait   où   le   drôle   était   allé."
Nobody   -not-   knew   where   the   joker   was   gone
                         had

"'Il   s'amuse   trop!'   dit   Pierre."
He   himself amuses   too much   said   Pierre

"Six   mois   après,   le   pauvre   père   sut   que   son
Six   months   afterwards   the   poor   father   knew   that   his
                         found out

fils allait être pris par la justice à Nantes. Il
son went to be taken by the justice at Nantes He
  was

fait la route à pied, y va plus vite que
made the journey on foot there (one) goes more quick than
  faster

par mer, met la main sur son fils et l'amène ici.
by sea puts the hand on his son and him takes here

Il ne lui demande pas: 'Qu'as-tu fait?'"
He not him asks not What have you done

"Il lui dit: 'Si tu ne te tiens pas sage
He him said If you not yourself keep -not- wise

pendant deux ans ici avec ta mère et avec
during two years here with your mother and with

moi, allant à la pêche et te conduisant
me going to the fishing and yourself leading
  behaving

comme un honnête homme, tu auras affaire à
like an honest man you will have business with

moi.' L'enragé, comptant sur la bêtise de ses
me The enraged one counting on the stupity of his
  The madman

père et mère, lui a fait grimace. Pierre,
father and mother him has made a face Pierre

là-dessus, lui flanque une mornifle qui vous a
there upon him flanks a thump which -you- has
            hits

mis Jacques au lit pour six mois. La pauvre
put Jacques to the bed for six months The poor

mère se mourait de chagrin."
mother herself died of sorrow
         almost died

"Un soir, elle dormait paisiblement à côté de
One evening she slept peacefully at (the) side of

son mari, elle entend du bruit, se lève, elle
her husband she hears of the noise herself raises she

reçoit un coup de couteau dans le bras. Elle crie,
receives a cut of knife in the arm She cries

on cherche de la lumière."
one search of the light
they

"Pierre Cambremer voit sa femme blessée; il
Pierre Cambremer sees his wife wounded he

croit que c'est un voleur, comme s'il y en
believes that it is a robber as if it there of it

avait dans notre pays, où l'on peut porter
had in our country where it one can carry

sans crainte dix mille francs en or, du
without fear ten thousand franks in gold from the

Croisic à Saint-Nazaire, sans avoir à s'entendre
Croisic to Saint Nazaire without to have having to hear oneself

demander ce qu'on a sous le bras."
to ask be asked this what one has under the arm

"Pierre cherche Jacques, il ne trouve point son
Pierre searches for Jacques he not finds at all his

fils. Le matin, ce monstre-là n'avait-il pas eu
son The morning this monster there did not have he not had

le front de revenir en disant qu'il était allé à
the face the courage of to return in saying leaving a message that he was gone to

Batz. Faut vous dire que sa mère ne savait
Batz Is necessary you to say that his mother not knew

où cacher son argent. Cambremer, lui, mettait
where to hide her money Cambremer he put

le sien chez monsieur Dupotet du Croisic."
-the- his at Mister Dupotet of the Croisic

"Les folies de leur fils leur avaient mangé des
The idiocies of their son them had eaten of the

cent écus, des cent francs, des
hundred ecus of the hundred franks of the
{silver coins}

louis d'or, ils étaient quasiment
louis of gold they were almost
{coin with king Louis of France}

ruinés, et c'était dur pour des gens qui avaient
ruined and it was hard for -of the- people who had

aux environs de douze mille livres, compris
at the abouts -of- twelve thousand pounds included
approximately

leur îlot. Personne ne sait ce que
their small island Nobody -not- knows this that

Cambremer a donné à Nantes pour ravoir
Cambremer has given at Nantes for to have back

son fils. Le guignon ravageait la famille."
his son The piece of bad luck ravaged the family

"Il était arrivé des malheurs au frère de
It was arrived of the misfortunes to the brother of

Cambremer, qui avait besoin de secours. Pierre lui
Cambremer who had need of help Pierre him

disait pour le consoler que Jacques et Pérotte
said to him comfort that Jacques and Pérotte

(la fille au cadet Cambremer)
the girl of the junior Cambremer
younger

se marieraient." "Puis, pour lui faire gagner
themselves would marry Then for him to make earn
would marry

son pain, il l'employait à la pêche; car Joseph
his bread he employed him at the fishing because Joseph

Cambremer en était réduit à vivre de son travail.
Cambremer of it was reduced to live of his work

Sa femme avait péri de la fièvre, il fallait
His wife had perished of the fever it was necessary

payer les mois de nourrice de Pérotte. La femme
to pay the months of nursing of Pérotte The wife

de Pierre Cambremer devait une somme de cent
of Pierre Cambremer had / owed a sum of hundred

francs à diverses personnes pour cette petite,
franks to various people for this small

du linge, des hardes, et deux ou trois mois à
of the linen of the clothes and two or three month at

la grande Frelu qu'avait un enfant de Simon
the large Frelu who had a child of Simon

Gaudry et qui nourrissait Pérotte."
Gaudry and who nourished Pérotte

"La Cambremer avait cousu une pièce
The Cambremer had sewed a piece (of gold)

d'Espagne dans la laine de son matelas,
from Spain in the wool of her mattress

en mettant dessus: A Pérotte."
in putting writing on it A Pérotte

"Elle avait reçu beaucoup d'éducation, elle
She had received much of education / education she

écrivait comme un greffier, et avait appris à lire
wrote like a clerk and had learned to read

à son fils, c'est ce qui l'a perdu."
to her son it is that which she has lost

"Personne n'a su comment ça s'est fait,
Nobody not has / has known how that itself is done

mais ce gredin de Jacques avait flairé l'or,
but this bandit -of- Jacques had smelled the gold

l'avait pris et était allé riboter au Croisic."
it had taken and was gone to riot / have fun at the Croisic

"Le bonhomme Cambremer, par un fait
The good man Cambremer by a happenstance

exprès, revenait avec sa barque chez lui. En
intentional / as if ordained returned with his boat at he In

abordant il voit flotter un bout de papier, le
approaching he sees to float an end / a piece of paper it

prend, l'apporte à sa femme qui tombe
takes   it brings   to   his   wife   who   falls
  stumbles

à la renverse en reconnaissant ses propres
to the   reverse   in   recognizing   her   own
  back

paroles écrites."
words   written

"Cambremer ne dit rien, va au Croisic,
Cambremer   -not-   said   nothing   goes   to the   Croisic

apprend là que son fils est au billard; pour
learns   there   that   his   son   is   at the   billiard table   for

lors, il fait demander la bonne femme qui
at the time   he   lets   ask   the   good   woman   who

tient le café, et lui dit: 'J'avais dit à Jacques de
holds   the   pub   and   her   says   I had   said   to   Jacques   of

ne pas se servir d'une pièce d'or avec quoi
not   -not-   himself   serve   of a   piece   of gold   with   which
not

il vous payera; rendez-la-moi, j'attendrai sur la
he   you   will pay   return it to me   I will await   on   the

porte, **et** **vous** **donnerai** **de** **l'argent** **blanc** **pour.'**
door and you will give of money white for
            not stolen for it

La **bonne** **femme** **lui** **apporta** **la** **pièce.** **Cambremer**
The good woman him brought the piece Cambremer

la **prend** **en** **disant:** **'Bon!** **et** **revint** **chez** **lui.'"**
it takes in saying Good and returned to him
    saying   his place

"Toute **la** **ville** **a** **su** **cela.** **Mais** **voilà** **ce** **que** **je**
All the town has known that But here this that I
The whole

sais **et** **ce** **dont** **les** **autres** **ne** **font** **que**
know and this of which the others not do (anything) but

de **se** **douter** **en** **gros."** **"Il** **dit** **à** **sa**
of themselves doubt in large He says to his
  to doubt in large (very much)

femme **d'approprier** **leur** **chambre** **qu'est** **en** **bas;** **il**
wife to clean up their room that is in low he
        downstairs

fait **du** **feu** **dans** **la** **cheminée,** **allume** **deux**
makes of the fire in the chimney lights two

chandelles, **place** **deux** **chaises** **d'un** **côté** **de**
candles places two chairs of one side of
        on one

l'âtre, et met de l'autre côté un escabeau."
the hearth and puts of the other side a stool
        on

"Puis dit à sa femme de lui apprêter ses
Then says to his wife of him to prepare his

habits de noces, en lui commandant de
long dresses of weddings -in- her commanding -of-
clothes of weddings

pouiller les siens. Il s'habille."
to dress up in the hers He gets dressed
      hers

"Quand il est vêtu, il va chercher son frère,
When he is clothed he goes to seek his brother

et lui dit de faire le guet devant la maison
and him tells of to make the look-out in front of the house

pour l'avertir s'il entendait du bruit sur les
for to inform if he heard -of the- noise on the

deux grèves, celle-ci et celle des marais de
two gravel beaches this one and and that of the marsh of

Guérande."
Guérande

"Il rentre quand il juge que sa femme est
He returns when he judges that his wife is

habillée, il charge un fusil et le cache dans le
dressed he charges a rifle and it hides in the

coin de la cheminée. Voilà Jacques qui revient;
corner of the chimney Here is Jacques who returns

il revient tard; il avait bu et joué jusqu'à dix
he returns late he had drunk and played until ten

heures; il s'était fait passer à la pointe de
hours he himself was made to pass via the point of
        had

Camouf. Son oncle l'entend héler, va le chercher
Camouf His uncle him hears hail goes him search
                        hailing

sur la grève des marais, et le passe sans
on the gravel beach of the marsh and him passes without

rien dire."
nothing to say

"Quand il entre, son père lui dit: 'Assieds-toi
When he comes in his father him says Seat yourself

là,' en lui montrant l'escabeau. 'Tu es,' dit-il,
there -in- him showing the stool You are says he

'devant ton père et ta mère que tu as
before your father and your mother that you have

offensés, et qui ont à te juger.' Jacques se mit
offended and who have to you judge Jacques itself set
started

à beugler, parce que la figure de Cambremer
to howl by-this that the face of Cambremer
because

était tortillée d'une singulière manière."
was twisted of a singular manner
in a

"La mère était raide comme une rame."
The mother was stiff as an oar

"'Si tu cries, si tu bouges, si tu ne te tiens
If you shout if you budge if you not yourself hold

pas comme un mât sur ton escabeau,' dit Pierre
-not- like a mast on your stool says Pierre

en l'ajustant avec son fusil, 'je te tue comme
in him adjusting at with his rifle I you kill like
aiming at him

un chien.' Le fils devint muet comme un poisson;
a dog The son became silent like a fish

la mère n'a rien dit."
the mother not has nothing said

"'Voilà,' dit Pierre à son fils, 'un papier qui
Here says Pierre to his son a paper which

enveloppait une pièce d'or espagnole; la pièce
wrapped a piece of gold Spanish the piece

d'or était dans le lit de ta mère; ta mère
of gold was in the bed of your mother your mother

seule savait l'endroit où elle l'avait mise; j'ai
only knew the place where she it had put I have

trouvé le papier sur l'eau en abordant ici;'"
found the paper on the water in approaching here

"'tu viens de donner ce soir cette pièce d'or
you come of to give this evening this piece of gold

espagnole à la mère Fleurant, et ta mère
Spanish to the mother Fleurant and your mother

n'a   plus   vu   sa pièce dans son lit.'"
not has anymore seen her piece   in   her   bed

"'Explique-toi.'"
Explain yourself

"Jacques dit qu'il   n'avait   pas pris la pièce de
Jacques   says that he did not have not taken the piece of

sa mère, et que cette pièce lui était restée de
his mother and that this piece him was left over from

Nantes."
Nantes

"'Tant mieux,' dit Pierre. 'Comment peux-tu nous
So much better says Pierre How can you us

prouver cela?' 'Je l'avais.' 'Tu n'as pas pris celle
to prove that I it had You not have not taken the one
                          have

de ta mère?' 'Non.' 'Peux-tu le jurer sur ta vie
of your mother Not Can you it to swear on your life

éternelle?' Il allait le jurer;"
eternal He went it to swear

"sa mère leva les yeux sur lui et lui dit:
her mother raised the eyes on him and him says

'Jacques, mon enfant, prends garde, ne jure pas
Jacques my child take guard not swear -not-
take care don't

si ce n'est vrai; tu peux t'amender,
if this is not true you can amend yourself

te repentir; il est temps encore.' Et elle
yourself repent it is time still And she
repent yourself there

pleura. Vous êtes une ci et une ça, lui dit-il,
cried You are a this and a that her says he

'qu'avez toujours voulu ma perte.'"
that have always wanted my loss
doom

"Cambremer pâlit et dit: 'Ce que tu viens de
Cambremer pales and says This what you come of

dire à ta mère grossira ton compte. Allons
to say to your mother will grow bigger your account Let us go

au fait! Jures-tu?' 'Oui.' 'Tiens,' dit-il, 'y avait-il
to the fact Swear you Yes Hold says he there had it

sur ta pièce cette croix que le marchand de
on your piece this cross that the merchant of

sardines qui me l'a donnée avait faite sur la
sardines who me it has given had made on the

nôtre?' Jacques se dégrisa et pleura."
ours Jacques himself sobered up and cried
himself disillusioned

"'Assez causé,' dit Pierre. 'Je ne te parle pas de
Enough babbled says Pierre I not you speak not of

ce que tu as fait avant cela, je ne veux pas
this that you have done before that I not want -not-

qu'un Cambremer soit fait mourir sur la place
that a Cambremer will be made to die on the place

du Croisic. Fais tes prières, et dépêchons-nous!
of the Croisic Do your prayers and let us dispatch us

Il va venir un prêtre pour te confesser.'"
It goes to come one priest for yourself to confesser
There

"La mère était sortie, pour ne pas entendre
The mother was gone out for not -not- to hear
had not

condamner son fils. Quand elle fut dehors,
condemn her son When she was outside

Cambremer l'oncle vint avec le recteur de Piriac,
Cambremer the uncle came with the rector of Piriac

auquel Jacques ne voulut rien dire. Il était
to which Jacques not wanted nothing to say He was

malin, il connaissait assez son père pour savoir
sly he knew enough his father for to know

qu'il ne le tuerait pas sans confession."
that he not him would kill not without confession

"'Merci, excusez-nous, monsieur,' dit Cambremer
Thank you excuse us sir says Cambremer

au prêtre, quand il vit l'obstination de Jacques.
to the priest when he saw the obstinacy of Jacques

'Je voulais donner une leçon à mon fils et vous
I wanted to give a lesson to my son and you

prier de n'en rien dire.'"
request of not of it nothing to say

"'Toi,' dit-il à Jacques, 'si tu ne t'amendes pas,
You says he to Jacques if you not yourself amend not

la première fois ce sera pour de bon, et j'en
the first time this will be for of good and I of it

finirai sans confession.'"
will finish without confession

"Il l'envoya se coucher. L'enfant crut cela et
He him sent himself lay down / to sleep   The child believed that and

s'imagina qu'il pourrait se remettre avec
himself thought that he could himself set back / make up with

son père."
his father

"Il dormit. Le père veilla."
He slept The father watched

"Quand il vit son fils au fin fond de son
When he saw his son at the end deep of his

sommeil, il lui couvrit la bouche avec du
sleep he him covered the mouth with -of the-

chanvre, la lui banda avec un chiffon de voile bien
hemp it him gagged with a rag of sail well

serré; puis il lui lia les mains et les pieds.
tightened then he him bound the hands and the feet

Il rageait, il pleurait du sang, disait Cambremer
He raged he cried of the blood said Cambremer

au justicier. Que voulez-vous! la mère
to the dispenser of justice What want you the mother

se jeta aux pieds du père."
herself threw at the feet of the father

"'Il est jugé,' dit-il, 'tu vas m'aider à le mettre
He is judged said he you go to help me to him put

dans la barque.'"
in the barque

"Elle s'y refusa. Cambremer l'y mit tout
She herself there refused Cambremer him there put all
      it

seul, l'y assujettit au fond, lui mit une
by himself him there fixes at the bottom him put a

pierre au cou, sortit du bassin, gagna la mer,
stone on the neck left of the basin gained the sea
  reached

et vint à la hauteur de la roche où il est."
and came at the height of the rock where he is

"Pour lors, la pauvre mère, qui s'était fait
For at the time the poor mother who herself was made
  had

passer ici par son beau-frère, eut beau crier
pass here by her brother in law had had well to shout

'Grâce!' ça servit comme une pierre à un loup."
Mercy that served like a stone to a wolf

"Il y avait de la lune, elle a vu le père
It there had of the moon she has seen the father

jetant à la mer son fils qui lui tenait encore
throwing at the sea her boy who she kept still
  in

aux entrailles, et comme il n'y avait pas
at the entrails and as it not there had not
in the womb

d'air elle a entendu blouf! puis rin, ni
of wind she has heard splash then noth'n neither

trace, ni bouillon; la mer est d'une fameuse
trace nor bubble the sea is of a famous
                                          a

garde, allez!"
keeper go
      go figure

"En abordant là pour faire taire sa femme
In approaching there for to make be quiet his wife

qui gémissait, Cambremer la trouva quasi morte;"
who groaned Cambremer her found half dead

"il fut impossible aux deux frères de la porter,
it was impossible to the two brothers of her to carry

il a fallu la mettre dans la barque qui
it has been necessary her to put in the boat which

venait de servir au fils, et ils l'ont
came of to serve for the son and they her have
  just was used

ramenée chez elle en faisant le tour par la
brought back at her in making the turn by the

passe du Croisic."
pass of the Croisic

"Ah! ben, la belle Brouin, comme on l'appelait,
Oh well the beautiful Brouin like one called her
                                        they

n'a pas duré huit jours; elle est morte en
not has not lasted eight days she is dead in

demandant à son mari de brûler la damnée
asking to her husband of to burn the damned

barque. Oh! il l'a fait."
boat Oh he it has done

"Lui, il est devenu tout chose, il savait plus
He he is become all thing he knew not anymore
                everything

ce qu'il voulait; il fringalait en marchant comme
this what he wanted he staggered in marching like
                                     going

un homme qui ne peut pas porter le vin."
a man who not can -not- carry the wine
                                his

"Puis, il a fait un voyage de dix jours et est
Then he has made a journey of ten days and is

revenu se mettre où vous l'avez vu, et,
returned himself put where you have him seen and
        to put himself

depuis qu'il y est, il n'a pas dit une
since that he there is he not has not said one
has

parole."
word

Le pêcheur ne mit qu'un moment à nous
The fisherman -not- put but a moment to us
used short time

raconter cette histoire et nous la dit plus
tell this history and us it told more

simplement encore que je ne l'écris.
simply still than I -not- it write

Les gens du peuple font peu de réflexions en
The people of the populace make little of reflexions in

contant, ils accusent le fait qui les a frappés,
telling they show the fact that them has struck

et le traduisent comme ils le sentent. Ce récit
and it translate like they it feel This account

fut aussi aigrement incisif que l'est un coup de
was as bitterly incisive that it is a blow of

hache.
axe

"Je n'irai pas à Batz," dit Pauline en arrivant
I will not go -not- to Batz says Pauline in arriving

au contour supérieur du lac.
at the contour / shore superior / upper of the lake

Nous revînmes au Croisic par les marais salants,
We returned to the Croisic by the marshes saline

dans le dédale desquels nous conduisit le
in the maze of which / through which us led the

pêcheur, devenu comme nous silencieux. La
fisherman become like us silent The

disposition de nos âmes était changée. Nous étions
disposition of our hearts was / had changed We were

tous deux plongés en de funestes réflexions,
all / both two plunged in -of- gloomy reflexions

attristés par ce drame qui expliquait le rapide
saddened by this drama which explained the rapid

pressentiment que nous en avions eu à l'aspect
presentiment that we of it had had at the aspect

de Cambremer. Nous avions l'un et l'autre
of Cambremer We had the one and the other

assez de connaissance du monde pour deviner
enough of knowledge of the world for to guess

de cette triple vie tout ce que nous en avait
of this triple life all this that us of it had

tu notre guide.
muted our guide
not told

Les malheurs de ces trois êtres se
The misfortunes of these three beings themselves

reproduisaient devant nous comme si nous les
reproduced before us as if we them

avions vus dans les tableaux d'un drame que ce
had seen in the scenes of a drama that this

père couronnait en expiant son crime nécessaire.
father crowned in expiating his crime necessary

Nous n'osions regarder la roche où était
We did not dare to look at the rock where was

l'homme fatal qui faisait peur à toute une contrée.
the man fatal who made fear to all a region

Quelques nuages embrumaient le ciel; des
Some clouds dimmed the sky -of the-

vapeurs s'élevaient à l'horizon, nous
vapors rose at the horizon we

marchions au milieu de la nature la plus
went at the middle of the nature the most

âcrement sombre que j'aie jamais rencontrée. Nous
pungently somber that I have never encountered We

foulions une nature qui semblait souffrante,
walked over a nature which seemed suffering

maladive, des marais salants, qu'on peut à bon
sickly of the marshes salt that one can with good
                salt marshes

droit nommer les écrouelles de la terre.
right call the eczema of the earth

Là, le sol est divisé en carrés inégaux de
There the ground is divided in squares unequal of

forme, tous encaissés par d'énormes talus de terre
form all encased by of enormous slopes of earth
enormous

grise, tous pleins d'une eau saumâtre, à la
gray all full of a water brackish at the

surface de laquelle arrive le sel.
surface of the-which arrives the salt
of which

Ces ravins, faits à main d'homme, sont
These ravines made with hand of man are

intérieurement partagés en plates-bandes, le long
internally divided in flat bands the length
causeways

desquelles marchent des ouvriers armés de longs
of which go of the workmen armed of long
the with

râteaux, à l'aide desquels ils écrèment cette
rakes with the aid of which they skim this

saumure, et amènent sur des plates-formes
pickle and bring on of the platforms
the

rondes pratiquées de distance en distance ce sel
rounds placed of distance in distance this salt
at equal distances

quand il est bon à mettre en mulons.
when it is good to put in heaps

Nous côtoyâmes pendant deux heures ce triste
We coasted during two hours this sad

damier, où le sel étouffe par son abondance
checkerwork where the salt chokes by its abundance

la végétation, et où nous n'apercevions de loin
the vegetation and where we did not see of far

en loin que quelques paludiers, nom donné à ceux
in far but some paludiers name given to those

qui cultivent le sel.
who cultivate the salt

Ces hommes, ou plutôt ce clan de Bretons
These men or rather this clan of Breton people

porte un costume spécial, une jaquette blanche
carry a costume special a jacket white

assez semblable à celle des brasseurs.
quite similar to that of the brewers

Ils se marient entre eux.
They themselves marry between them
marry

Il n'y a pas d'exemple qu'une fille de cette
It not there has not of example that a girl of this
There's no example

tribu ait épousé un autre homme qu'un
tribe has married an other man than a
any

paludier.
paludier
salt marsh worker

L'horrible aspect de ces marécages, dont la
The horrible aspect of these marshes of which the

boue était symétriquement ratissée, et cette terre
mud was symmetrically raked and this earth

grise dont a horreur la Flore bretonne,
gray of which has horror the Flora Breton

s'harmonisaient avec le deuil de notre âme.
harmonized with the mourning of our heart

Quand nous arrivâmes à l'endroit où l'on passe
When we arrived at the place where it one passes
one

le bras de mer formé par l'irruption des eaux
the arm of sea formed by the irruption of the waters
the intrusion

dans ce fond, et qui sert sans doute à
in this deep and which serves without doubt to

alimenter les marais salants, nous aperçûmes avec
feed the marshes salt we saw with
salt marshes

plaisir les maigres végétations qui garnissent les
pleasure the thin vegetations which decorated the

sables de la plage. Dans la traversée, nous
sands of the beach In the crossing we

aperçûmes au milieu du lac l'île où
saw at the middle of the lake the island where
in the

demeurent les Cambremer; nous détournâmes la
lived the Cambremer we diverted the

tête.
head

En arrivant à notre hôtel, nous remarquâmes un
In arriving at our hotel we noted a

billard dans une salle basse, et quand nous
billiard in a room low and when we

apprîmes que c'était le seul billard public qu'il
learned that it was the only billiard table public that it

y eût au Croisic, nous fîmes nos
there had with the / at Croisic we made our

apprêts de départ pendant la nuit; le
preparations of departure during the night the

lendemain, nous étions à Guérande.
following day we were at Guérande

Pauline était encore triste, et moi je ressentais
Pauline was still sad and me I felt

déjà les approches de cette flamme qui me
already the approaches of this flame which me

brûle le cerveau.
burns the brain

J'étais si cruellement tourmenté par les visions que
I was so cruelly tormented by the visions that

j'avais de ces trois existences, qu'elle me dit:
I had of these three existences that she me said

"Louis, écris cela, tu donneras le change à la
Louis write that you will give -the- change to the

nature de cette fièvre."
nature of this fever

Je vous ai donc écrit cette aventure, mon cher
I you have thus written this adventure my dear

oncle; mais elle m'a déjà fait perdre le calme
uncle but she me has already made lose the calm
it

que je devais à mes bains et à notre séjour ici.
that I owed to my baths and to our stay here

Fin
End

www.ingramcontent.com/pod-product-compliance
Lightning Source LLC
La Vergne TN
LVHW051236080426
835513LV00016B/1626